# JOHNSON FAIN PARTNERS

Selected and Current Works

# JOHNSON FAIN PARTNERS

Selected and Current Works

First published in Australia in 1997 by
The Images Publishing Group Pty Ltd
ACN 059 734 431
6 Bastow Place, Mulgrave, Victoria, 3170
Telephone (61 3) 9561 5544 Facsimile (61 3) 9561 4860

National Library of Australia Cataloguing-in-Publication Data

     Johnson Fain Partners: selected and current works.

     Bibliography.
     Includes index.
     ISBN  1 875498 77 X.

     1. Johnson Fain Partners. 2. Architecture, Modern—20th
     century—United States. 3. Architecture, American. 4. Architects
     —United States. (Series: Master architect series 3).

720.92

Edited by Stephen Dobney
Designed by The Graphic Image Studio Pty Ltd,
Mulgrave, Australia
Art direction by Anita Moryadas
Film by Scanagraphix Australia Pty Ltd
Printed in Hong Kong

# Contents

# Contents continued

# INTRODUCTION

# Introduction

## Johnson Fain Partners:
## The Princes of Baroque Modernism

*By Aaron Betsky*

Markers that stand in a landscape of sprawl, spaces that make sense in that same urban collage: this is the work of Johnson Fain Partners. Rich in allusions and open-ended in execution, theirs is work that brings a sense of Baroque complexity to the thoroughly modern situations it houses.

Scott Johnson and Bill Fain make objects and spaces that act as markers in a landscape to which order comes through grids, axes, and the episodic application of geometry. They work separately, one concentrating more on the making of architecture, the other on the design of the urban spatial structures in which such architecture can appear, yet they share a particular perspective on how we should be ordering our world. It is an attitude based on a belief in technology, rationality, and streamlined functionality in response to a society dominated by a capitalist system.

Yet this provides only the basic structure of their work. Onto this they layer, often quite literally in the form of a building skin or landscape grid, a way of ordering our environment that draws on history, the landscape, and the individual. At its best, the work of Johnson Fain Partners is a beautiful tapestry, condensed into a singularly expressive form. Though their architecture does not redefine the boundaries of the design profession, it does represent some of the most sophisticated syntheses of the many forces at work in the production of the world we inhabit.

Two features mark the accomplishments of these designers: an interest in the principles and aesthetics of the incomplete, and the strength of the resulting singular images. For Scott Johnson, this sense of the incomplete is most evident in buildings whose skins seem to be unfinished. The Nestlé USA Headquarters in Glendale, California[3], for instance, appears as a bundle of shooting stalks of glass and stone veneer, while 1999 Avenue of the Stars in Century City[1] seems to stretch itself taut around a corner, so that the building appears from some angles like a quarter of an implied circle. Sometimes, such frayed constructions are jarring and expressive, as in the case of the Andrex Vermont Gateway[4], whose simple form pulls apart at the center, as if its top

1

2

and bottom were about to take a ride down the adjacent Harbor Freeway in opposite directions. In Fox Plaza, the incompletion resolves itself as the building profile ascends: a complex star pattern floor plan that could keep spiraling around forever, so that the tower looks both variegated and unified from different angles.

One can say the same for the work at a more intimate scale, where Johnson brings together materials and domestic typologies that would seem to be in conflict. The berm surrounding the classical rotunda of the Opus One winery in Napa Valley, California[2] comes apart at the center to allow entry into a courtyard where what could be the scaffolding for the stone becomes a trellis on the balcony level above, while the missing part of the circle reappears as the great sweep of the *cave* on the level below. In Johnson's own house nearby,[5] the shifting planes of the house are like regularized contour lines or massive versions of the rows of grapes which define the immediate area. These planes indicate views down towards the valley, leaving the living spaces, almost as an afterthought, in between their walls. The priorities of Frank Lloyd Wright's Ennis House, the obvious model for the residence, become tellingly reversed: it is not space and order that are dominant, but rather the indication of lines of possibilities, and the etching of geometries on a landscape that is not completely replaced.

Such a sense of implication and indication also surfaces in the work of Bill Fain. One suspects that there it has its roots in Fain's long-standing efforts in participatory community design. He worked for a decade with neighborhood groups and governmental agencies to renovate, reassemble, and otherwise order troubled neighborhoods. He does similar work for a different constituency in his current practice. Here the neighborhoods are often either undeveloped sites or areas that some centralizing force (such as a redevelopment agency or city council) wants to control and define.

Whatever the client, Fain does not impose a complete urban form: geometries grow out of particular markers and landscape cues, and weave themselves together into something that appears not so much as one place but as a collage of different orders. Thus the city of Kapolei in Hawaii[6] found its organizing element in the local ancient monuments, inspiring neighborhoods that have a sense of coherence and community. The Indian Wells projects[7] started as a series of landscape views that Fain then translated into grids or lines of palm trees; simple lawns and lines in the desert that indicated a principle to what had been orderless sprawl. Yet the desert remained always present as the datum line that underlay and validated these moments of sense.

Perhaps the most complete assertion of Fain's ability as a weaver of urban form is his Greenways Plan for open space in Los Angeles.[8&9] Instead of dreaming of grand avenues or new forms, Fain sought connectors that were already present in the Los Angeles basin: disused rail and trolley lines, power line rights-of-way, flood control basins, and areas too geologically unstable to be developed. Together these pieces and strings formed a dense, interconnected network. Fain drew these lines out into green spaces, which, he pointed out, could be used for recreation, farming, and public transportation, rather than as building sites. The proposal works as an antidote to the centrifugal sprawl of Southern Californian urbanism.

One senses the presence of Los Angeles in the work of Johnson Fain Partners. Though neither architect was trained there, they seem to have assimilated its lessons well. Perhaps whatever order Los Angeles possesses comes from the continual transformation of its abstract landscape through overlays of technology. This proposition is echoed in the firm's projects which acknowledge LA's changing collage of man-made forms through the insertion of clear but open-ended structures. Their designs act as responsive markers in a diffuse and complex landscape.

6  EWA TOWN CENTER
ESTATE OF JAMES CAMPBELL              PEREIRA ASSOCIATES              TOWN CENTER SITE PLAN
                                                                              JULY. 1986

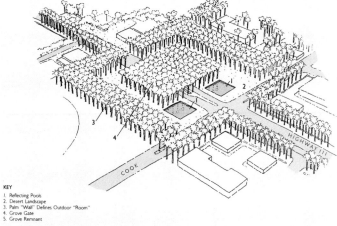

KEY
1. Reflecting Pools
2. Desert Landscape
3. Palm "Wall" Defines Outdoor "Room"
4. Grove Gate
5. Grove Remnant

7

Certainly there is a direct line here: this firm is, after all, the successor to one of the central players in the game of transforming urban collage into institutional form. William Pereira brought a sense of grand history — the kind that makes monuments — to a Modernist practice, thus giving the central institutions of his community a sense of what they could be. Pereira's forms were never comfortable or complete, and thus were never accepted as high-style exemplars of architectural virtue by the arbiters of taste of his day. To a certain extent, Johnson Fain Partners find themselves in a similar place, making an architecture about a social project they did not create.

What is instead especially remarkable in both Johnson's and Fain's work is that they use the traditional tools of architecture and urban design as instruments rather than as closed systems. Their designs are like a corporate version of the "collage city" proposals first put forward by Colin Rowe in the 1970s. Modernism to them means not only abstract forms and functional construction, but the complete availability of all history, all techniques, and all forms. The act of the designer is to collect these inherited fragments, frame them, and reposit them as something that is not unitary, but evocative and indicative of future possibilities of interpretation and use. This does not mean that the work is chaotic, but that it is open-ended.

In the case of Johnson's buildings, that process extends beyond the work of the designer. Fox Plaza, for example, has been transformed from an office building, first into an urban marker that has become a landmark for commuters and tourists, and then into "the *Die Hard* building" by its use as the set for the film of that name.[10] Though Johnson admits to some uneasiness about this latter development, it highlights the multiple personalities built into the building, which draws on vaguely Moorish geometries in plan to evoke some of the exotic exuberance of the original

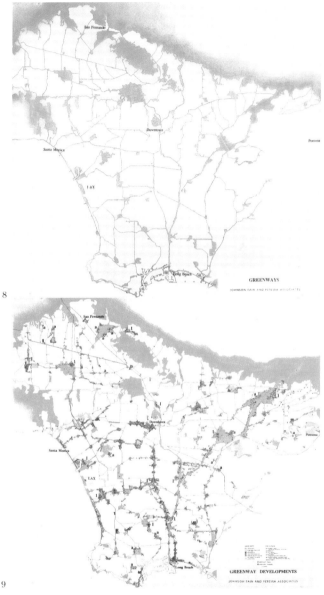

8

9

skyscrapers of the 1930s. By making a marker that does not have any direct references, but opens itself up to many associations, Johnson created the possibility for the assimilation of a speculative office block by popular culture.

Bill Fain's work evokes popular images of small towns and dense urban situations in episodic pieces that have none of the heavy-handed direct "theming" that one might expect from either the Disney Corporation or the so-called New Urbanists. The juxtaposition of the shopping street that Fain inserted alongside Pereira's Modernist central circle at the University of California at Irvine increases the intensity of each of these separate myths of how students are meant to live in the prototype community of the American college campus. A recent proposal for China Basin in San Francisco mixes the metaphors of a small traffic circle, a Baroque "circus," and Times Square.[11] It promises to create an urban node that is an extension both of the commercial realms that bind our cities together and of the kind of small-scale "place-making" that is essential in newly planned neighborhoods.

There is, to be sure, a certain Baroque quality about the work of Johnson Fain Partners. Like the Baroque designers of the 16th century in Italy, the firm inserts its markers and fragments of grids as the controlling devices that announce the presence of one organizing force or power. Like Baroque designers, Johnson and Fain delight in the sense of the unfinished or *infinito*, which implies both the limitless possibilities of construction itself and the sense of mortality or entropy that is intrinsic to any system of construction.

As a result, both the future and the past are implicit in the work of Johnson Fain Partners. Their buildings and places are very much of the moment, delighting in the possibilities that technology, sites, and clients give them, while accepting both the

10

11

treasure-trove and the restrictions of what the past has prepared for them, and indicating possible transformations, either by the lines of the building or by the sites prepared for future architects after the urban plan has been made. Their work is a complication and relaxation of the dictates of Modernism that still uses its economic, stylistic, and logical structure; such a response is Baroque in nature.

These are delightful weavings that help make sense of a physical environment whose threads are increasingly more loosely woven, rather than master works demanding continual attention and a belief in their principles. Whether it is the enigmatic urban marker of Fox Plaza or the hopeful lines of the Greenways Plan,[12] the work of Johnson Fain Partners indicates a richly sedimented and allusive order that will have to be completed, preferably by the viewer or user, in a future in which these two accomplished designers still believe.

*Aaron Betsky is the Curator of Architecture and Design at the San Francisco Museum of Modern Art. A designer and critic, he is the author of seven books on architecture including* Violated Perfection: Architecture and the Fragmentation of the Modern *and* Icon: Magnets of Meaning. *Mr Betsky is a contributing editor of* Architecture, Blueprint, ID, *and* Metropolitan Home.

12

The Princes of Baroque Modernism    15

# Introduction

## Johnson Fain Interview

*Aaron Betsky*
*Describe some of your early professional experiences which eventually lead to joining Bill Pereira in Los Angeles. What kind of experience or ideas did you bring with you, why did you choose this office, and how did it come to have its current structure?*

*Bill Fain*
After UC Berkeley, I worked for Ian McKinley in the Bay Area. I was designing mid-scale housing projects, and I asked myself how I could really address the environment when I was just dressing up boxes. So I got a fellowship to go to England and studied with F.J. McCulloch at the University of Manchester. That started a pattern of finding a new professional experience every two years.

From England I went to work for Jacque Robertson in Mayor John Lindsey's office in New York, on the Fifth Avenue Special Zoning District, which was the first legislated mixed-use district of its kind. Then we proposed closing Madison Avenue to vehicular traffic. I also worked on other special-purpose districts such as the Theater District.

While in England, I focused on the ideas of Milton Keynes new town, north of London. Its planning was based on the idea of "permissive planning" — a kind of Americanization of the English new town — put forth by Mel Webber in the late 1960s.

Following England, I went to the Graduate School of Design at Harvard, while I also worked for the Boston Redevelopment Agency. I worked for Stuart Forbes on planning [the area] around Fanuiel Hall, which was being formulated at the time, and I helped design the first incentive planning district downtown. Then I worked in Richmond before winding up at the New Communities Development Corporation under President Carter.

We worked on a program by which we sponsored neighborhood groups to do job training by working on their own houses and apartments. We were substituting labor for capital. We went to twenty-eight different cities, did a lot of research, analyzed it from a client's point of view, and then proposed our own line of funding to those communities. That's where I really got started on research; I realized the importance of gathering all these statistics and background information. I was really beginning to understand how you don't just design boxes, but how you can affect your environment by understanding the basic ingredients behind what you are designing: economics and social issues, politics, capital, labor, context. The hope is that you develop an understanding about what will work for a community when you do that.

I moved back to Los Angeles, where I grew up, in 1980. I felt that there was little institutional context here, and realized that one must fall back on an ability to draw, to connect. I thought that I could turn that drawback into an asset. I went up to see Bill Pereira, and we sat down with my portfolio at two o'clock, and I walked out of the place at quarter to eight. It turned out that he had this great interest in urban design as creating environments, or setting up situations in which others can actually design: frameworks. He was intrigued by the idea of structuring a process. After a year of talking, I joined the firm, and six months later it was announced that there would be a change in the way the firm was organized.

### Scott Johnson

After I graduated, I worked and taught in Boston, Los Angeles, and San Francisco for a while. Then I moved to New York to work for Philip Johnson. When I was in my twenties, Philip Johnson's office interested me because of the adventure-someness of the ideas he undertook at that time, which was the late 1970s. But what was also happening was that he had a lot of huge work. I wasn't focused on that, but I ended up, in six years, working on a lot of big, big buildings. I was comfortable with that because I was interested in the problems of dimension and scale, as well as in the civic and institutional issues relating to the user groups and the client bodies.

Then Bill Pereira asked me to become the design partner in his office. I really didn't know him. I didn't come to Los Angeles because I revered the work. I just knew that I was working in scale and I needed an infrastructure to operate in scale and this seemed to be one office that had been well-regarded. I knew I couldn't do tall buildings, for example, out of my garage. When Bill eventually passed away and the office had to be completely revamped, Bill Fain and I, who had been classmates at Harvard, came together and we said, well let's do this together, because one of us alone isn't going to make this happen. At that time the office was very low on work, but Fox Plaza, when it was completed, was so successful on several levels that within three months several more sizable projects came in and kind of gave us our first independent life. Bill was working on Kapolei and I was working on Fox Plaza and was beginning on Rincon Center and the Opus One winery. Fox Plaza was frankly so successful that it allowed us to take over the firm, changing its name and its ownership.

**Aaron Betsky**

*Scott, would you say that in the partnership, you come from a more Modernist, abstracting school of thought?*

**Scott Johnson**

Without question. Bill approaches research in a way which is actually quite different from me. Usually, I am interested in history only in terms of its chronology of physical typologies and their relation to the history of ideas. With such a strategic or narrow approach, I am free to abstract elements forward from the past like the Modern architect that I am. Bill has a very different process to mine, both by dint of our different orientations, but also in terms of the scale of the ventures.

**Aaron Betsky**

*Bill, how do you collaborate with Scott?*

**Bill Fain**

When Scott and I first started working together, he asked a very interesting question, which was: "Do you like to be given a program to design from, or do you like to have an open-ended program?" I prefer an open-ended program, and he is exactly the opposite, because he wants to design buildings, while I find that the idea or the innovation can take place in the redefinition of the problem inherent in the program.

My work is involved with a different set of information, but in terms of values there is a lot of similarity in how things come out. How we actually work together depends on the project. On 1999 Avenue of the Stars, for instance, we had some very interesting discussions, because I was interested in how a building can tell you something about a city. This was on a site very different from that of Fox Plaza, which is right near there. It was a corner site, and we had to figure out how to make the building engage that corner. The curved building we came up with marks the site. It's a corner piece waiting for other buildings to come up and help complete the block.

**Aaron Betsky**

*Can you give me an example of the kind of research you do?*

**Bill Fain**

On the Kapolei project, which was a master plan for a 6,000-acre area west of Honolulu on Oahu, we sent Katherine Rinne to research the history of urbanization of the islands. We realized that urbanization was antithetical to the way people live in the Hawaiian Islands: they live in nature, not in the city. So we had to find a rhythm for that kind of life. Katherine spent the whole time at the Bishop Museum, and she mapped all the mythological sites in the area. There were almost fifty of them, and they grounded the narrative of the new town we proposed.

We found that in historic Honolulu there was a kind of place where the natives and the Americans used to gather every afternoon and have a drink together and find out the news about each other, and we incorporated that as well in the Kapolei plan. We always like to use archaeological references, because it gives a meaning to the landscape. We try to discover the central idea for each project.

**Aaron Betsky**

*It sounds as if the two of you are trying to set up a Modernist-versus-historicist pole, and yet it doesn't seem quite that simple. Scott, for instance, when I think of your work I see an attempt to take the technology of current corporate architecture and make it figurative, to give it a shape and a presence. Whether it's the Opus One winery, which is a very strong figure in the landscape, or Fox Plaza, or even the Vermont Gateway building on the Harbor Freeway, it's all about this very gestural presence.*

**Scott Johnson**

Well, I would agree, but I would say it a different way. I would describe Fox Plaza in terms of its essential abstract bone structure. I would describe the Opus One winery as a helix inserted midway in the ground that suggests a certain ambiguity between being on the ground and of the ground. I would suggest that that's a fundamental abstract notion — it's not narrative in the sense that the building is not a wine glass, the building is not a barrel.

As for the rhomboidal building on the Harbor Freeway, there's a notion there about trying to take an all-too-simple program, which is that of a speculative office building, and impute into its shape and its skin the kinetics of the freeway it abuts. That's why it has that diagonal grid, which I hope looks as if it is moving, rather than static and married to its place. I would call that the fundamental sculptural, formal quality of the building, and yet I always try to understand the geometries so that they imply some inherent ambiguity.

But yes, I'm clearly interested in modern things. I'm interested in the whole series of dialectics that would be more related to the art world and art-making and less concerned with recapitulating history or style periods.

**Aaron Betsky**

*Bill, you would not describe yourself as a New Urbanist, would you?*

**Bill Fain**

I'm not wedded to any particular school. I'm focused on looking for the idea, the innovation, or the invention behind a particular problem. The central idea behind a project often has to do with the open space. For example, when we did UC Irvine "Main Street," I realized that the circle in Pereira's original master plan had a nice garden sense to it, but lacked a certain sense of place. So we tried to develop a traditional street in the context of that loosely defined ring of buildings. It set up a nice dialectic between suburbia and a denser urban environment.

**Aaron Betsky**

*It seems as if you both look at urban agglomerations as being always in process, rather than possessing a fixed order, and that your work comes out of that perception.*

**Bill Fain**

Yes. Our work is very process-oriented. It comes out of the city, rather than being something we import. That was the idea behind the LA Open Spaces project: those spaces were drawn to connect to each other so that they would create more harmonious places. I try to find the "Pareto-optimal" solutions in a process that involves clashing interests. Vilfredo Pareto was an early 20th century Italian philosopher who talked about situations in which few loose and someone can gain. I believe that if you can resolve issues in a neutral way and make everyone better off at the same time, you're in a pretty optimal situation.

**Aaron Betsky**

*Scott, in your case there seems to be an ambiguity between what one would associate with a traditional, Beaux-Arts approach to place- or form-making and a kind of Modernist collage. Is that conscious?*

**Scott Johnson**

That may be a result of the process. When I do a building I will frequently just think about fundamental physical properties of what it seems the building is likely to be. Sometimes you can't put your finger on it that quickly, but maybe the building is going to be tall and narrow, or maybe the building is going to be long and low, or infinitely long, or maybe it's going to be a strange blob. Then I like to go back to look through history or read through the libraries to find, for instance, other long, low, flat things. That may get me to Baroque palaces or that may get me to some prehistoric things, not because their architectonic language is necessarily relevant, but because I'm just interested in how they deal with those overriding properties.

Those will be references and keys, but I would say that I don't consciously approach design in a Beaux-Arts way. When I was in New York I was particularly interested in modern sculptors like Donald Judd and Carl Andre and Sol Lewitt and Richard Serra. I think that's something that has continued through the last ten years and probably keeps getting stronger.

**Aaron Betsky**

*At what point does it become difficult to make sculpture? When a building gets above a certain size, doesn't the relationship between the body and the building become rather difficult?*

**Scott Johnson**

Probably it does. I'm not sure what that scale is. Certainly there are things to commandeer and focus on when you get bigger and bigger and bigger. I would wonder whether that point is defined by the context in which that architectural event exists. For example, a tall building in Hong Kong would be very different from a tall building in Reno or some other more anonymous place. I do think, going back to the wall problem though, in the end the thing has to have haptic scale.

In the end there is still a human body that moves through space, that comes upon a building, that approaches it from far away. It gets closer to it, it can touch it, and it can finally enter it. That process is still limited, constrained, or defined by the dimensions of the body.

**Aaron Betsky**

*Bill, you work on so many large projects, yet few of them ever are realized. Does that ever frustrate you?*

**Bill Fain**

The large-scale plan takes a long time to implement. To be successful, it needs to structure design decisions within the planners' framework. One must assume many designers of buildings will work within the framework. To that extent, you have to build in a level of incompleteness. You try to establish the principles that, over time, will develop.

**Aaron Betsky**

*Are the clients for the kind of large buildings for which your firm became famous getting harder to find?*

**Scott Johnson**

Yes. Business entities more than ever feel that they might be merged: they are ultimately liquid. If they monumentalize a huge amount of their capital into a physical asset like a building, they need to be able to liquidate that building at any time. I don't think the huge urban building is necessarily dead for all time, but you ask yourself a whole other series of questions now. That doesn't mean that there isn't scale, there isn't volume, and there isn't monolithic capital. It's just that everyone's worried about the bottom line.

**Aaron Betsky**

*When you work in a place like Asia, do you feel as if you come with a "value-neutral" approach to a site, or how do you tie it to a particular place?*

**Scott Johnson**

How do you define a place that works in that environment of world wide capital and electronic communication which is non-physical, and at the same time create something that is going to be regionally responsive? That's just too big a question to answer, unless we're talking about Kyoto, we're talking about 1994, and a certain neighborhood. Then you can begin to define appropriate spheres or platforms for regionalism. I think that gets you into issues that really unite architecture and urban design in a very tight dialogue. Urban design becomes fundamental as a tool in that discussion.

**Aaron Betsky**

*A great deal of the firm's work now is in Asia. How do you feel about working there?*

**Bill Fain**

As markets become larger and more global, one of the biggest problems we have in the late 20th century is that capital formations tend to create bigger and bigger projects. Scale becomes a central issue. Urban design tends to be expressed in large buildings: monolithic platforms with theme parks, many millions of square feet of retail and towers on top. The problem that Southeast Asia has to confront, given this situation, is to create something at a humane scale in these monolithic, highly capitalized projects.

History has shown that even though a project is of considerable scale, it can be broken down to relate in a human way to the street — for example, Raymond Hood's design for Rockefeller Center. He respected the scale of the block and brought the perceived size of the towers down by faceting them and scaling them back to the level of a five-story brownstone. The grid structure gives you a basic ingredient, as does the integrity of the structural system. You can then use all of these pieces to resolve the conflict inherent in such large-scale structures.

**Aaron Betsky**

*How would you characterize the public approval process that you encountered in many of the large corporate campuses or private developments that marked your work in the 1980s?*

**Bill Fain**

I don't believe you ever do truly private work. The truth resides somewhere between public good and private gain. In the late 1980s, the process for doing plans and even just single buildings became more and more complicated. That's where we come in. We put ourselves in the position of either a community person or the city. We try to incorporate their needs in our projects. In doing so, Scott and I both feel that a project is often better off for being part of a public process.

The conflicts that come out of that process can become part of the narrative and make the project better. We learned how to take very large private projects while inserting public benefits into them. In that way we helped the approval process and defined the programs along the way.

**Aaron Betsky**

*Bill, you seem to be interested in the notion of a narrative to a plan, and you also have a very imagistic sensibility. You seem to look for a story or an evocative image in all the situations for which you plan.*

**Bill Fain**

Let me give you an example. When we did the Indian Wells project, we tried to understand the desert, not just in statistics, but as a place with its own nature. That was why people moved there originally, for that place. We looked at the historic paintings of the desert from the Plein Air period, and they helped us to capture the essence of that landscape. In all the paintings we looked at, there were three clear ingredients: the desert plane, the mountains, and the sky. We used those three basic elements in each aspect of our proposal. We worked with an illustrator to create a series of nine scenes that you might see as you drove along the highway in our planning area. By doing so, we tried to capture the intangible qualities of the desert. They came together with the tangibles, the statistics, in a very beautiful way. That is really the objective, to get those two together.

**Aaron Betsky**

*Does it all come back down to the importance of place-making?*

**Bill Fain**

A lot of it does. The essence of urban design is creating these urban places. They can be spaces for exchange and commerce, or they can be monumental and passive spaces. I am intrigued by the idea that not all spaces are already defined. In all the plans we do, there is an element of anarchy and the unresolved. They contain a little bit of organized chaos. That is perhaps the intangible that we try to marry to the tangibles of development. Out of the nearness of that chaos, we try to create a sense of engagement that ultimately gives you a sense of harmony.

*Aaron Betsky*

*Is visualization technology fundamentally altering the shape of buildings or is it just another tool?*

**Scott Johnson**

In terms of the information systems available to communicate and conceptualize architecture, it's enormously different now than it was just a few years ago. You can't even imagine that you could practice the way you did three or five years ago with what's available today. But in terms of buildings, there's still a universalism to building materials which has to do with structures: concrete, steel, skin, whatever … and light, that is evolving, but I think it's moving much slower than the technologies that define communication.

At the same time, we are seeing the popular information-generated redefinition of what matters in architecture. The ascendancy of the entertainment studios and the networks underscores that. Right now we think: "Electronic information is so much at our fingertips, isn't that wonderful?" Well, yes and no. It's creating a popularization which can reduce everything to a very simplistic and frequently sentimental narrative, rather than allowing the thing to exist as an abstract idea.

The entertainment industry, which is wildly successful today, is about storytelling and that's about narrative and that, in turn, might be about the sentimental or popular attachment you have to a building, among other things.

I'm really interested in the process of abstraction and that's fundamental to how I see myself in my time. Abstraction is a way to move away from sentiment, to distill fundamental structures and allow buildings to work over time; to have a reality or credibility over time.

I think that all industries and cultures right now are struggling with the increasing loss of the individual voice. I want to continue to hammer on that idea and try to find a venue for expressing my particular contribution there. In the last couple of years I've been getting more small buildings to design: I'm receiving commissions for remodels, interiors, houses, and wineries. With that work, I want to create vehicles for channeling some of this monolithic capital and the institutions that deal with that large scale into unique, intimate, and very humane buildings.

# SELECTED AND CURRENT WORKS I

# 1999 Avenue of the Stars

Design/Completion 1987/1990
Century City, California
JMB Urban Development Company
820,000 square feet
Steel frame, granite, high-performance glass curtainwall, limestone, marble, stainless steel

1999 Avenue of the Stars, a 38-story tower, is located at the geographic center of Century City at the intersection of Constellation Boulevard and Avenue of the Stars. Focusing attention on this central intersection, the project's dynamic elevations vary in silhouette and transparency and are highly visible from surrounding areas of west Los Angeles. The building's exterior skin is composed of various layers of green and golden granite, custom aluminum window frames, and various tinted solar glasses. Glass areas in both flat and broadly curved walls increase the viewing range of perimeter offices in the tower.

The building's elevation at this focal point of Century City is strategically designed to welcome the unusually high flow of pedestrian traffic. A dramatic triple-height space surrounds the lobby whose interior walls are finished in sanded limestone, with green pinstriped granite paving and black French marble. Finishes in the public interior space are monumental and classical.

The entry from the parking garage is fully weather-protected and has its own elevator core and convenience retail support. To the north is a generous motor court paved in granites and landscaped with a grove of pollarded sycamore trees. On the sunny southern side, a park with an adjacent restaurant accommodates lunch-time activities.

1

2                  3                  4                  5

1999 Avenue of the Stars            29

6

7

8

9

10

11

1999 Avenue of the Stars

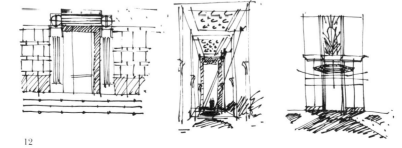

12

# Rincon Center

Design/Completion 1986/1989
San Francisco, California
Perini Land & Development Co.
1 million square feet
Precast concrete exterior, reinforced concrete
Custom glass curtainwall, natural stone detailing

Rincon Center is a mixed-use urban project occupying a full city block at the heart of San Francisco's downtown, one block from the Bay. The project comprises the adaptive re-use of the historic Rincon Postal Annex and existing public lobbies, food court, retail gallery and office space, and the design for new construction of an outdoor plaza, ground-level retail and restaurants, mid-rise office space, and two residential towers of 160 units each.

1

The primary design goal was to establish a clear circulation hierarchy that provided a natural procession from each element to the next. Rincon Center's primary movement diagram is cruciform in plan. This system allows penetration into the complex from each perimeter street, separates new and existing construction, and brings coherence to the entire project. The new construction to the rear of the historic Annex is designed as an articulated concrete shell; its natural stone base, window configurations, and cornices complement the rhythms and finishes of the existing landmark. The two residential towers above are outwardly curved to create shared rather than competing views, and to orient the units to the Bay.

2

3

4

5

Rincon Center

6

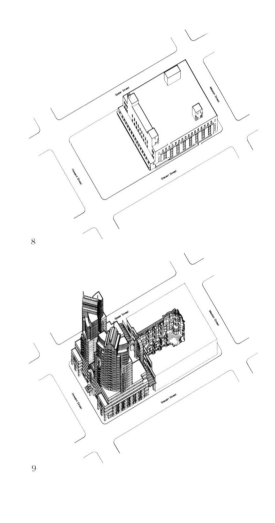

8

9

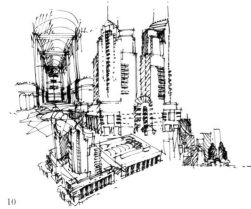

10

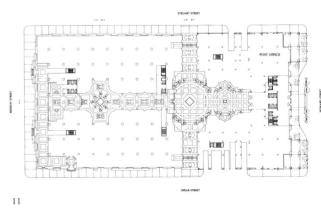

11

12

13

14

15

Rincon Center

16

17

18

19

20

21

Rincon Center

# Rockefeller Center Conceptual Retail Study

Design 1990
New York, New York
Rockefeller Center Management, Inc.
500,000 square feet

Rockefeller Center, developed in the 1930s by John D. Rockefeller, was designed as a "city within a city": a mixture of business, culture, and supporting services. The center was expanded in the 1970s with the addition of four office buildings along the west side of Sixth Avenue. Originally designed as stand-alone structures with no direct pedestrian linkage, these buildings lack a successful retail environment. Currently, only an indirect pedestrian route exists through the subway concourse.

This study focuses on retail uses at the street and concourse levels, and builds upon existing and proposed pedestrian circulation. Street level plazas are clarified by removing landscape and hardscape obstacles and infilling over existing basement level courtyards. The improved concourse level integrates with access to the existing Sixth Avenue subway station as well as to the proposed Seventh Avenue station. All four buildings are linked by a below-grade retail pedestrian street which is operated by a single management organization. Glass atria house escalators for access between the street and concourse levels and also provide natural light. The center includes a full range of services and entertainment uses.

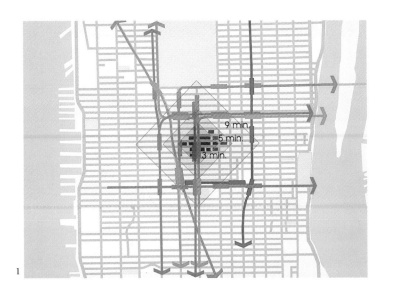

1

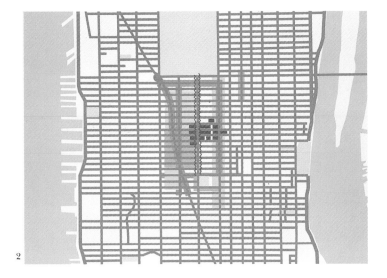

2

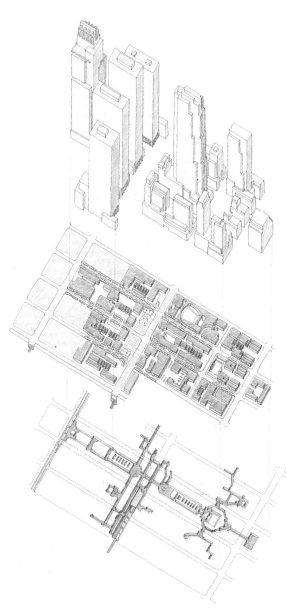

Rockefeller Center
Conceptual Retail Study

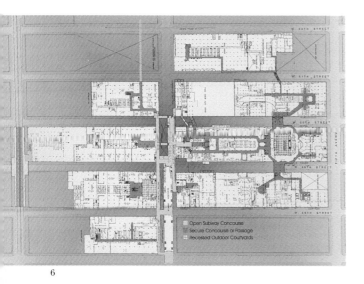

6

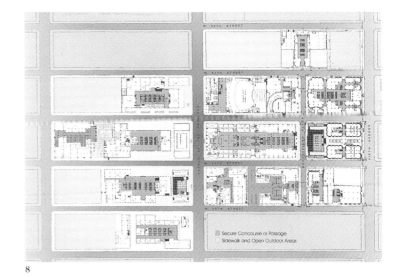

8

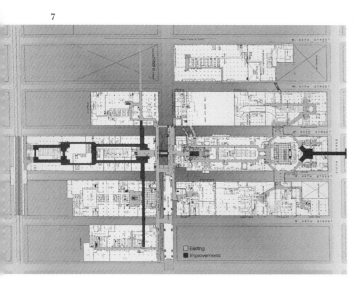

7

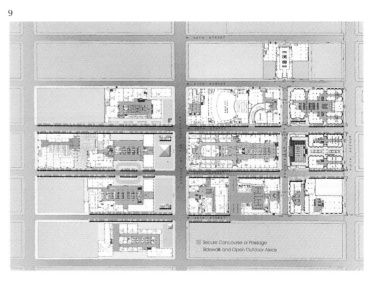

9

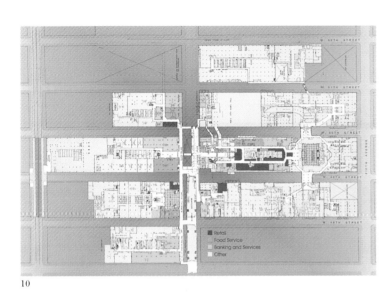

10

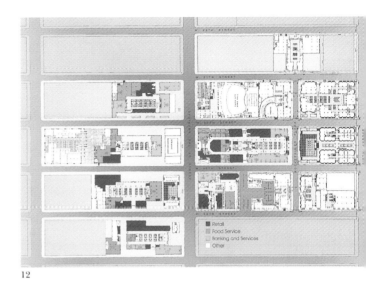

12

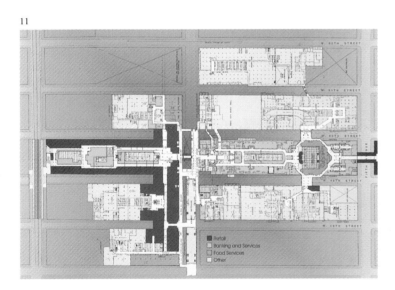

11

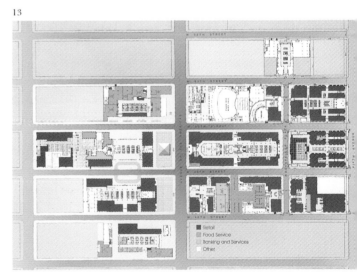

13

Rockefeller Center
Conceptual Retail Study

41

# Los Angeles Center

Design 1986/1989
Los Angeles, California
Hillman Properties, Smith and Hricik Development Co.
5.2 million square feet (master plan); 1.6 million square feet (Phase I)
Steel frame, granite, high-performance glass curtainwall

Los Angeles Center is a new urban destination which acknowledges the westward movement of the downtown business core. The project comprises a total land area of 18 acres, 6 acres of which form a series of public open spaces; a total built area of 5.2 million square feet; and below-grade parking. By virtue of its size and strategic location, Los Angeles Center has the potential to redefine opportunities for mass transit, open space, and automobile and pedestrian routes to existing residential neighborhoods and the downtown financial core.

Landscaped circulation paths, surrounded by continuous retail and food services, connect thematic open spaces. Out of the roughly hewn stone bases grow faceted high-rise towers, sited diagonally to optimize the use of natural light. Floor plate sizes are large and the faceting of the building provides a multitude of corner offices per floor.

The primary automobile arrival at the motor court of the Phase I twin towers was designed in collaboration with Martha Schwartz, landscape architect. Ground level pedestrian entry is marked by a 120-foot-long curved lobby with a hanging glass and steel window wall designed by James Carpenter.

1

1   Model of Phase I twin towers
2   Aerial view of motor court and entry
3   Photomontage of development in downtown
    Los Angeles
4   Sketches (Scott Johnson)

Los Angeles Center

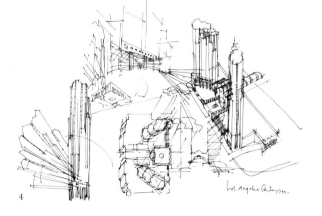

5

6

7

8

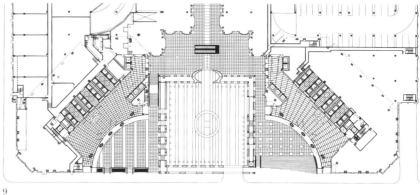

9

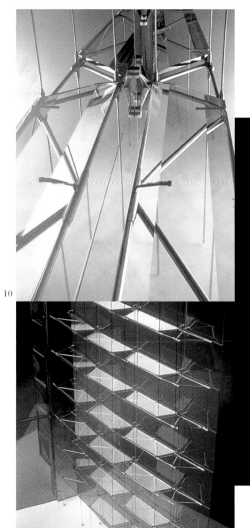

10

11

12

Los Angeles Center

# Fox Plaza

Design/Completion 1985/1987
Los Angeles, California
MKDG/20th Century Fox Film Corporation
Improvements 1996: LaSalle Partners
650,000 square feet
Steel frame
Granite, high-performance glass

Fox Plaza is a 34-story tower encompassing 650,000 square feet of office space, sited on axis with Olympic Boulevard, one of Los Angeles' most heavily traveled east–west arteries.

Designed to accommodate offices for 20th Century Fox Film Corporation, Fox Plaza explores the ambiguity of reading pure forms in architecture at a monumental scale. The building's mass comprises the assembly of two square shafts rotated and merged, thus offering varying displays of natural light depending on the sun's orientation. This play of light on the facade is further enhanced by the changing granite-to-glass ratio, transparency increasing with height.

The building's skin (composed of granite polychromy at the base) expresses a repetitive horizontality appropriate for its office program throughout the midspan, and presents a highly transparent silhouette at the top for ease of recognition at a distance.

In 1989 Fox Plaza featured prominenently in the 20th Century Fox motion picture *Die Hard*.

Fox Plaza

47

6

7

Fox Plaza

# Nestlé USA Inc. Headquarters

Design/Completion 1987/1990
Glendale, California
Lincoln Properties/Nestlé USA Inc.
525,000 square feet
Steel frame, granite, high-performance glass curtainwall

1

This headquarters building for Nestlé USA Inc. marks the northern end of Glendale's Brand Boulevard. The building is sited to allow its publicly accessible, 37,000-square-foot garden to occupy the primary corner. This formal garden provides benches, shade trees, water events, and planted arbors, and is a usable and generous forecourt to the building. The plaza side of the building is symmetrical in plan and has a formalized axial entryway designed in the tradition of European *parterres* — ornamental gardens with flowering beds and paths formed in geometric patterns. The northern side of the project, which abuts the irregular Los Angeles River, is asymmetrical in plan and has an eccentric rear garden. The adjacent parking has a carefully designed facade which completes the composition and provides views over the garden beyond.

At the building's base are food product laboratories and testing kitchens, a 400-seat cafeteria with private garden, and a multimedia conference center which is available to the community after hours. Public lobbies have custom lighting, articulated plaster ceilings and soffits — all in a rich palette of dark wood veneers — polychromed stone floors, and a mixture of stainless steel and bronze finishes.

2

3

4

Nestlé USA Inc. Headquarters

51

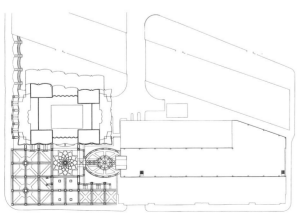

5

6

8

9

10

7

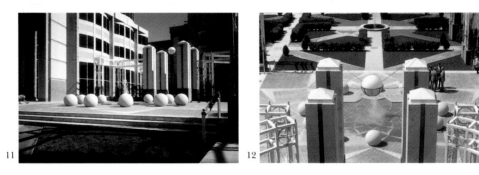

11

12

13

# The New Wilshire

Design/Completion 1983/1986
Los Angeles, California
The Bracton Corporation
200,000 square feet
High-performance glass, neoprene window wall,
stainless steel, granite, marble

The New Wilshire is a mid-rise office tower
in Los Angeles' Miracle Mile district.
Located at the intersection of Wilshire
Boulevard and Fairfax Avenue, home to
the historic May Company building and
the Petersen Automotive Museum, the
building responds in plan and elevation
to the trapezoidal geometry of its site.

The building's massing accentuates the
site's unique shape. The elevations'
shifting planes are punctuated by a series
of stainless steel balconies, emphasizing
the prismatic quality of the building's
form. The balconies also allow natural
light and air into the building's interior.

The New Wilshire acts as a beacon at its
important location.

1

1  Entry and north elevation
2  Window wall and south elevation
3  Balcony detail
4  Typical floor plan

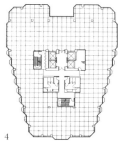

The New Wilshire

# Andrex Vermont Gateway

Design/Completion 1987/1989
Los Angeles, California
Andrex Development
260,000 square feet
Custom aluminum and glass curtainwall system

Andrex Vermont Gateway, a mid-rise office headquarters complex, sits prominently at the confluence of three major freeways in Southern California. The facade, with its shifted geometries and colors, acts like a three-dimensional supergraphic, suggesting the effect of highway speed on a building.

A spacious entry rises from the building's two-story base. The building artfully recomposes the distinctions between the base, middle, and crown of traditional office tower design. The mid-section of the building is characterized by a dark grey parallelogram which peels away to reveal the lighter colored portion of the building.

1

Andrex Vermont Gateway

# Bunker Hill Towers

Design 1987
Los Angeles, California
First Street Properties
600,000 square feet (Phase I); 400,000 square feet (Phase II)
Steel frame
Granite, high-performance glass curtainwall

The Bunker Hill Towers are located on Grand Avenue at the top of Bunker Hill in downtown Los Angeles on land owned by Los Angeles County. The brief called for a two-phased project which conformed to the height restrictions, setbacks, and public circulation patterns defined in the Los Angeles Downtown Strategic Plan.

The design is for a pair of mixed-use office towers with retail and public open space. By articulating a small-scale, digitally inspired grid within a larger rectangular super-grid, the design facets the vertical shaft of the high-rise towers. The two buildings nest diagonally to provide open views and allow sunlight into the central open area within the block.

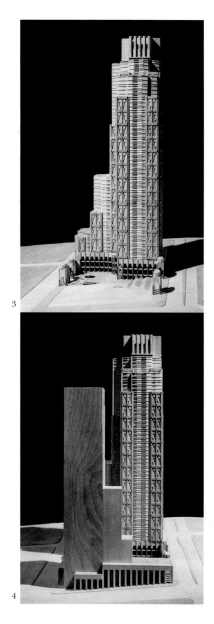

1

2

3

4

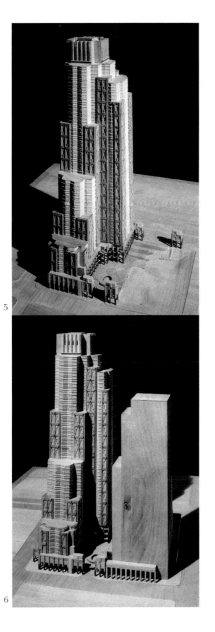

5

6

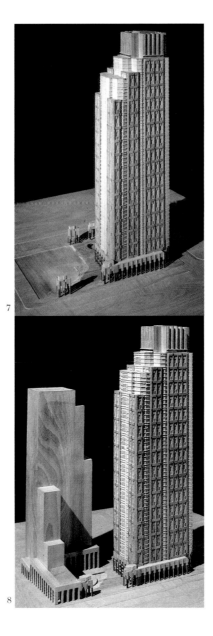

7

8

Bunker Hill Towers

# Sunflower City

Design 1995
The Sunflower Group
Bangkok, Thailand
990 acres (master plan)
85 million square feet (building program)

Sunflower City is a proposed satellite mixed-use business district situated on 990 acres on the outskirts of Bangkok. The master plan program totals 85 million square feet of building area and includes a new Bangkok Railway Station and Northern Bus Terminal; a World Trade Center district with specialized facilities for global trading and financial services; and an international Exhibition and Convention Center. Sunflower City also includes a technology center with university-level academic and corporate facilities oriented toward advanced telecommunications technologies; a retail/entertainment center with high-technology entertainment facilities; and extensive retail and commercial operations.

The plan provides residential districts, parks, and community amenities structured around a new internal circulation system and an existing central park.

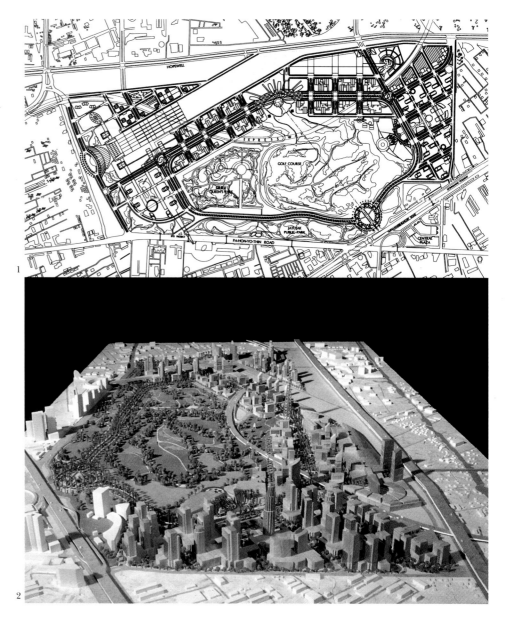

1

2

3

Sunflower City

4

5

6

7

Sunflower City

# Trump Wilshire Tower

Design 1990
Los Angeles, California
Trump Wilshire Associates
6,000,000 square feet

This mixed-use project for a 23-acre site in the historic mid-Wilshire Boulevard district of Los Angeles includes a design for a 145-story super-tall office tower. With a complex express elevator core and exoskeletal moment frame structural system, the building offers three million square feet of high-rise office space. Stepping back on three sides as the building ascends, the highly faceted window wall establishes a landmark profile on the skyline.

The remainder of the project site includes a major hotel with banquet facilities, a variety of residential unit types, and more than one million square feet of retail with space for anchor tenants. The site plan establishes an internal boulevard edged with retail that terminates in the destination hotel and recreational decks at the rear of the site. The tower, located near the center of the deep site, allows lower-scale buildings to form a gateway from Wilshire Boulevard and frame a view to the hotel beyond.

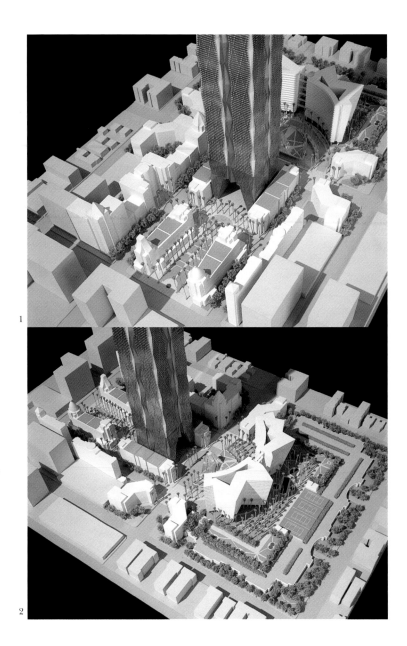

1

2

1 Aerial view of gardens on Whishire Boulevard
2 Aerial view of hotel and recreational gardens
3 Tower elevation detail
4 Tower model
5 Tower elevation studies

3

4

Trump Wilshire Tower

65

5

# Trump Wilshire Center

Design 1991
Los Angeles, California
Trump Wilshire Associates
6,000,000 square feet; 23 acres

This master plan for a prominent 23-acre site on Wilshire Boulevard includes a design for approximately six million square feet of mixed-use commercial development. The project is organized around a newly created boulevard, which extends from Wilshire Boulevard into the site.

The resort complex includes six office towers, ranging from 30 to 60 stories in height, organized along the internal boulevard which terminates at a 400-room atrium-style conference hotel. The boulevard has a mix of support retail, entertainment and performance facilities, and food service. At the edges of the site, abutting residential zones, are a variety of residential building types. The complex is accessible from two subway stations along Wilshire Boulevard.

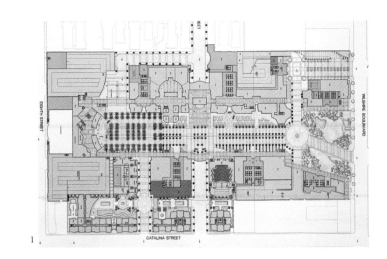

1

2

Trump Wilshire Center

8

9

10

11

12                                              13

Trump Wilshire Center                          69

# Los Angeles Civic Center Enhancement Plan

Design 1996
Los Angeles, California
Los Angeles Civic Center Authority
In collaboration with Meléndrez Associates, Public Works Design,
RAW International, Landmark Partnership
280 acres

Los Angeles has the second largest government center in the United States. The Enhancement Plan proposes a new pedestrian-oriented civic center for the city, recalling the traditional focus of the *pueblo*, with a mix of governmental, cultural, historic, business, and open space uses within a ten-minute walking diamond of the landmark City Hall building.

The Enhancement Plan recognizes the original patterns of development and provides for the reinforcement or re-introduction of historic building and land features. The plan identifies currently vacant or available sites for public and private development and encourages the sharing of government facilities, the adaptive re-use of historic buildings, the development of new open space, the integration of new cultural and historical elements into the Civic Center, and the promotion of public–private partnerships. The plan also includes increased pedestrian amenities and an improved streetscape.

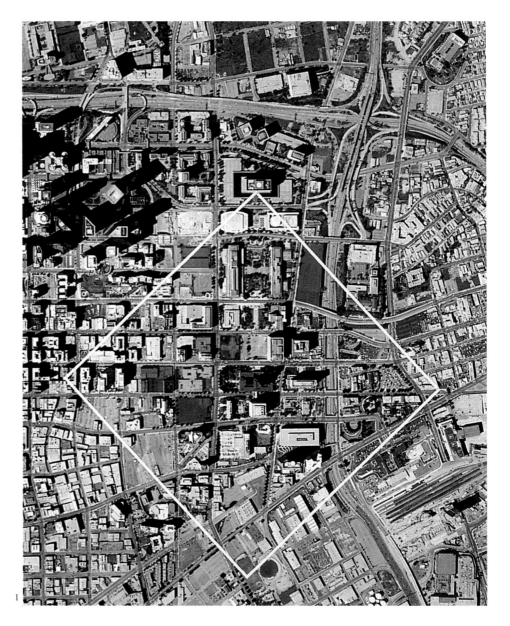

## $\mathscr{L}$ E G E N D

1. Angels Flight
2. Los Angeles City Hall
3. Hill Street Corridor
4. Japanese-American
   National Museum
5. MTA Headquarters
6. MWD Headquarters
7. Broadway State Building
8. Reagan State Building
9. Roybal Federal Building
10. Times Mirror Square
11. Union Station
12. Cathedral of Our Lady of
    the Angels
13. Disney Concert Hall
14. Geffen Temporary
    Contemporary Museum
15. El Pueblo Plaza
16. Los Angeles Mall
17. Main Street Bridge over
    Santa Ana Freeway
18. LAPD Headquarters
19. Civic Square
20. Civic Commons
21. Civic Gardens
22. New housing (possible
    sites)

*Hillside Quarter*

*El Pueblo Quarter*

*New Town Quarter*

*Riverbed Quarter*

2

Los Angeles Civic Center
Enhancement Plan

3

4

5

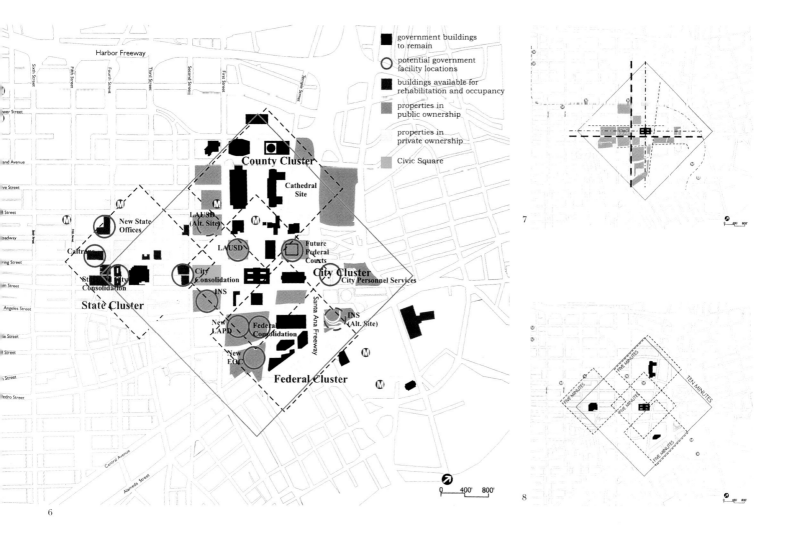

government buildings
to remain

potential government
facility locations

buildings available for
rehabilitation and occupancy

properties in
public ownership

properties in
private ownership

Civic Square

Harbor Freeway

County Cluster

Cathedral
Site

New State
Offices

LAUSD
(Alt. Site)

LAUSD

Future
Federal
Courts

City Cluster
City Personnel Services

Caltrans

City
Consolidation

State City
Consolidation

INS

State Cluster

New
LAPD

Federal
Consolidation

INS
(Alt. Site)

New
EOC

Federal Cluster

Santa Ana Freeway

Central Avenue

Alameda Street

0    400'   800'

6

7

8

0   400   800

0   400   800

FIVE MINUTES

FIVE MINUTES

FIVE MINUTES

FIVE MINUTES

TEN MINUTES

6   Four government sectors with priority sites
7   Major axes and strategic sites
8   Five- and ten-minute walking diamonds
9   Proposed street walls
10  Visual landmarks and open space
11  Recommended land uses

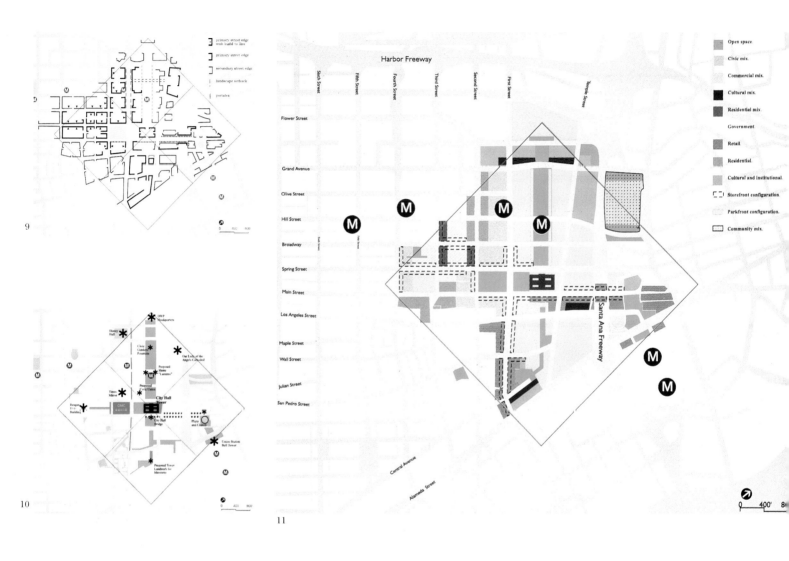

9

10

11

# Patramas Adhiloka Oil Plaza

Design/Completion 1995/1996
Jakarta, Indonesia
Pt. Patramas Adhiloka
4.1 million square feet

Patramas Adhiloka Oil Plaza, located in Jakarta's Golden Triangle, is designed as an international business center. The plan combines luxury high-rise residences with exclusive, class-A commercial office towers in an integrated development. The central 65-story building will house the headquarters of the national oil company. Retail, recreational, and landscape amenities are connected at the ground level by shaded arcades and thematic gardens of native plants.

With project massing and building silhouettes positioned to establish prominence and protect view corridors, the architectural treatments strive to capture a sense of modern-day Indonesia through the use of unique, culturally inspired features at each building's base and top.

The overall development program includes 2.7 million square feet of office and retail uses, and 640 condominiums and serviced apartments encompassing 1.4 million square feet. The residential mix includes one- to four-bedroom units and penthouse units with enhanced amenities.

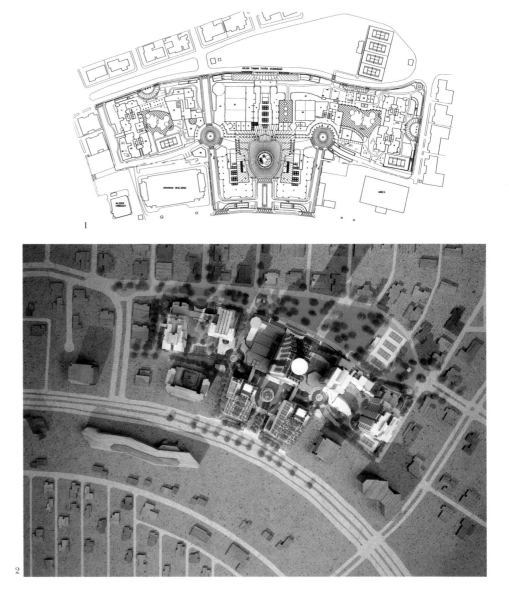

1

2

Patramas Adhiloka Oil Plaza

7

Patramas Adhiloka Oil Plaza

# Mission Bay Master Plan

Design 1997
San Francisco, California
Catellus
240 acres

The Mission Bay Master Plan proposes a mixed-use urban neighborhood which integrates and enhances San Francisco's existing street framework and open space system. The master plan, which covers the largest undeveloped site in San Francisco, allows for the rehabitation of land previously dedicated to locomotive transport and industrial uses.

The proposed block dimensions and orientation were informed by studies of block structures in cities with distinctive waterfront conditions, such as San Francisco, Seattle, and New York. The resulting block structure is small enough to encourage pedestrian flow and large enough for viable economic development. Block dimensions are based upon the historic "vara" unit of measurement, which was used in the layout of the original San Francisco grid. (One vara equals 2.75 feet.) The orientation of the streets provides view corridors to both the downtown business district and the Bay.

The framework of open space and landscape is a critical element of the plan and will complete and enhance the Waterfront Land Use Plan of the Port of San Francisco. Anchored by the central, 43-acre campus of the University of California San Francisco Medical Center, the Mission Bay Master Plan strives to integrate commercial and university uses with a balanced mixture of residential development, including affordable housing.

1

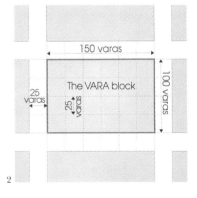

2

1 Rendered site plan
2 The vara block
3 Open space system
4 Building edges
5 Land use
6 View corridors
7 Neighborhoods
8 Historic *pueblo* lands and original
  San Francisco grid
9 New York grid orientation and view corridors
  to waterfront
10 Seattle grid orientation and view corridors
  to waterfront
11 San Francisco grid orientation and view
  corridors to waterfront

3

4

5

6

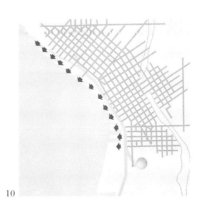

7

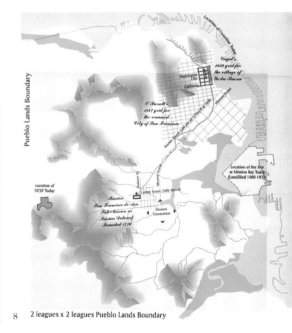

8  2 leagues x 2 leagues Pueblo Lands Boundary

Mission Bay Master Plan

79

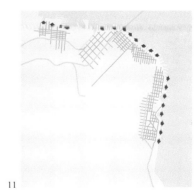

9

10

11

12

13

14

15

Mission Bay Master Plan

16

17

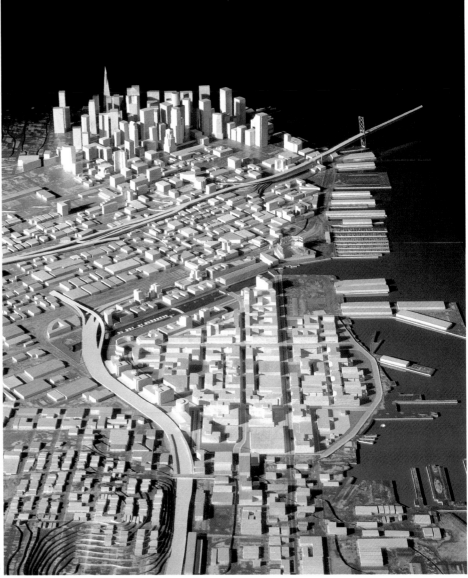

18

19

20

Mission Bay Master Plan

21

# The City of Kapolei

Design 1986
Oahu, Hawaii
Estate of James Campbell
6,000 acres

The City of Kapolei is officially designated as Hawaii's secondary urban center and is the largest and most significant planning project undertaken since statehood. Located 14 miles from downtown Honolulu, the 6,000-acre site includes 6 million square feet of commercial space and 12,000 housing units.

The urban design creates a new town which is distinctly Hawaiian in character. It is scaled for the pedestrian and oriented to views toward the ocean (*makai*) and the inland mountains (*mauka*). Organized around a city grid, the plan encourages elements of traditional Hawaiian culture such as the use of indigenous lava, coral, and bluestone building materials, and traditional building elements such as atria, roofed balconies, arcades, and courtyards.

The design was preceded by substantial research into the mythological, archaeological, and historical context of the region; especially significant locations have been made key public places. Based on historical research, the open space system re-establishes the Hawaiian *loku*, small parks designed for casual recreation and informal gatherings.

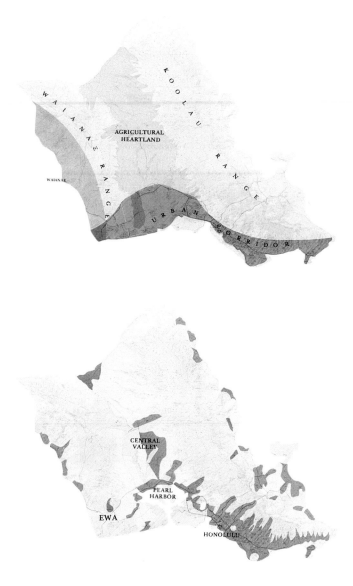

1

2

1   Spheres of influence: agricultural heartland,
     southern urban edge, coast
2   Existing urban areas
3   Kapolei town center plan
4   Land use plan

1.  Kapolei Park
2.  Kapolei Loku
3.  Guest House
4.  Wai-Aniani Lake
5.  Recreation Center
6.  Community Center
7.  Museum
8.  Main Center
9.  Makakilo Retail Center
10. Campbell Office Building
11. Campbell Blvd.
12. Campbell Mall
13. Corporate Headquarters
14. Kapolei Palms Hotel
15. Government Center
16. Town Hall
17. La 'Akona Colleg.
18. West Gate
19. East Gate
20. Hidani Footpad
21. Arenda Loku
22. Promenade Street
23. Lincob Park
24. Apartments
25. Townhouses
26. Single-Family
27. Palaial Tamphitheater
A.  H - 1 Freeway
B.  Makakilo Drive
C.  Farrington Blvd.
D.  Farrington Hwy.
E.  Fort Barrette Road
F.  Koolina Drive
G.  La 'Akona Blvd.
H.  Waimanalo Blvd.
I.  Waimanalo Parkway

3

The City of Kapolei

4

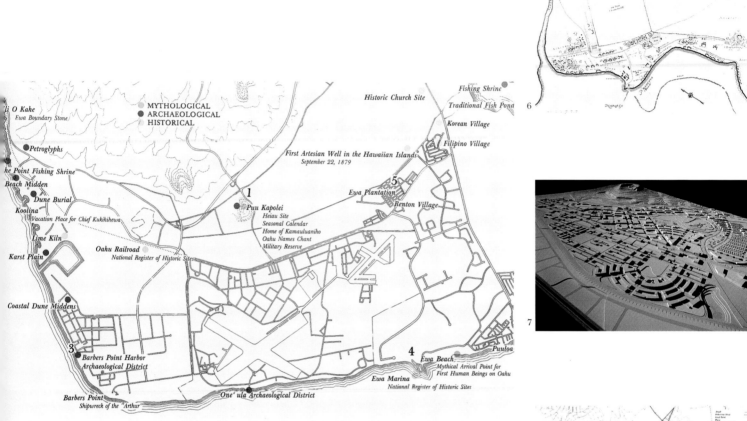

i O Kahe
*Ewa Boundary Stone*

MYTHOLOGICAL
ARCHAEOLOGICAL
HISTORICAL

*Historic Church Site*

*Fishing Shrine*

*Traditional Fish Pond*

6

*Petroglyphs*

*Korean Village*

*First Artesian Well in the Hawaiian Islands*
*September 22, 1879*

*Filipino Village*

he Point Fishing Shrine

Beach Midden

Dune Burial

*5*

*Ewa Plantation*

1

*Renton Village*

Koolina
*Vacation Place for Chief Kukihihewa*

*Puu Kapolei*
*Heiau Site*
*Seasonal Calendar*
*Home of Kamauluaniho*
*Oahu Names Chant*
*Military Reserve*

Lime Kiln

Karst Plain

*Oahu Railroad*
*National Register of Historic Sites*

Coastal Dune Middens

*Puuloa*

4

*Ewa Beach*
*Mythical Arrival Point for*
*First Human Beings on Oahu*

3

*Barbers Point Harbor*
*Archaeological District*

*Ewa Marina*
*National Register of Historic Sites*

Barbers Point
*Shipwreck of the "Arthur"*

*One'ula Archaeological District*

5

7

8

9

10

11

The City of Kapolei

12

# Los Angeles Open Space: A Greenways Plan

Design 1994
Los Angeles, California
Pacific Earth Resources
400 linear miles

Los Angeles is largely a post-war phenomenon: a young city lacking the layering and patina of older cities. Its residential districts are dominated by the single-family detached home; open space is overwhelmingly devoted to streets or private residential yards, rather than public plazas, parks, and parkways.

Since the 1950s, the growth of Los Angeles City and County has been enormous. This growth surge has all too often emphasized privatization of land and resources rather than humane development of a shared environment. While mitigating improvements in traffic, roads, and services have become commonplace, transit and transportation planning are not yet sufficiently coordinated with parallel efforts in land-use planning.

The Los Angeles Open Space concept provides a substantial increase in public open space by using available land resources such as transit lines, bikeways, rail rights-of-way, rivers, flood control channels, and powerline easements. The plan links a number of these land resources to existing town centers, schools, libraries, post offices, and senior centers while providing new sites for other uses. The concept can be the catalyst for the establishment of additional public parks, squares, and plazas, increasing the amount of open space available for public use and enjoyment.

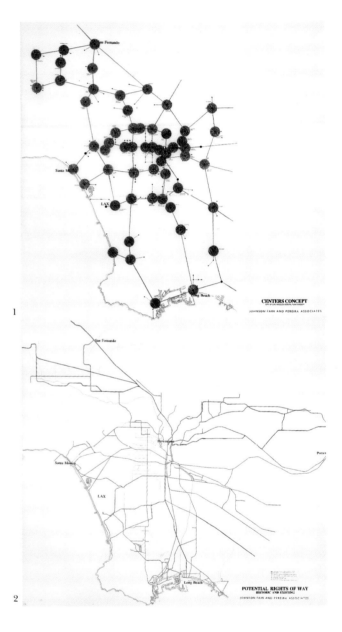

1  CENTERS CONCEPT
JOHNSON FAIN AND PEREIRA ASSOCIATES

2  POTENTIAL RIGHTS OF WAY
HISTORIC AND EXISTING
JOHNSON FAIN AND PEREIRA ASSOCIATES

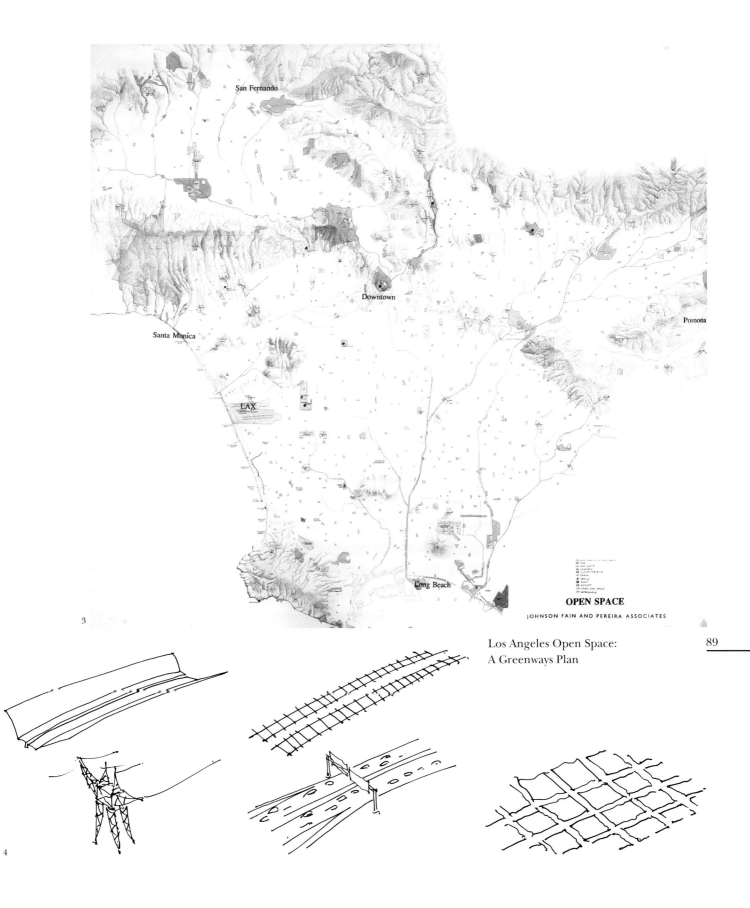

1   Urban centers within metropolitan Los Angeles
2   Potential rail rights-of-way
3   Existing open space and river courses
4   Continuous elements (flood control channels and
    river courses, powerlines, rail rights-of-way,
    freeways, city grid) (William Fain)

San Fernando

Downtown

Santa Monica

Pomona

LAX

Long Beach

**OPEN SPACE**

JOHNSON FAIN AND PEREIRA ASSOCIATES

3

Los Angeles Open Space:
A Greenways Plan

4

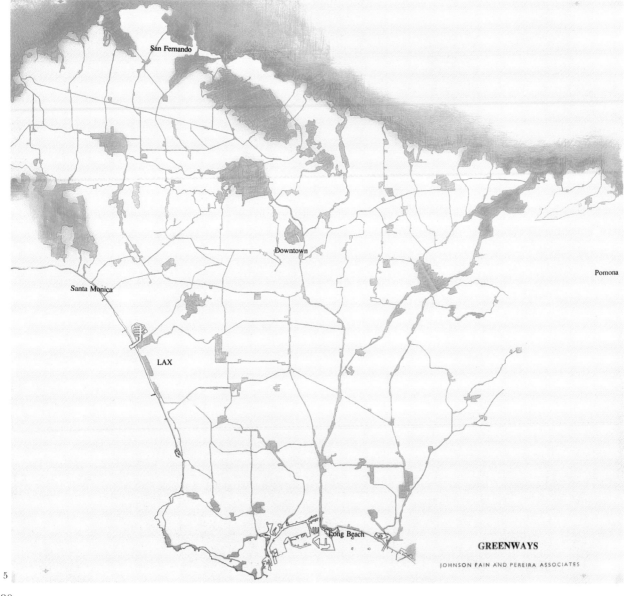

San Fernando

Santa Monica

Downtown

Pomona

LAX

Long Beach

**GREENWAYS**

JOHNSON FAIN AND PEREIRA ASSOCIATES

6

GREENWAY DEVELOPMENTS

JOHNSON FAIN AND PEREIRA ASSOCIATES

Los Angeles Open Space:
A Greenways Plan

7

8

9

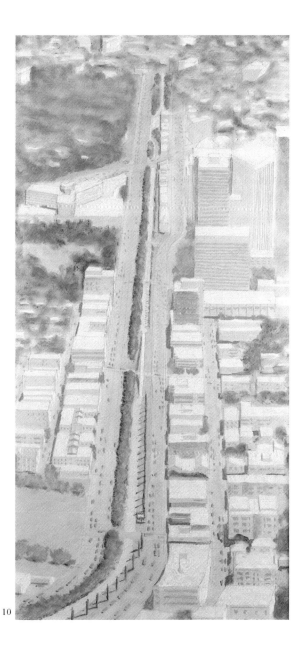

10

11

Los Angeles Open Space:
A Greenways Plan

12

# SELECTED AND CURRENT WORKS II

# Indian Wells Specific Plan

Design 1988
Indian Wells, California
City of Indian Wells

The Indian Wells Specific Plan, which covers a 3.5-mile highway corridor in the small desert community of Indian Wells, rescinds existing strip retail zoning in favor of traditional desert landscape and residential, resort, open space, and community/institutional uses.

The plan establishes a landscape zone on both sides of the highway. In keeping with large-scale resort, hotel, and recreational development areas, the north landscape zone includes formal arrangements of date palms in multiple rows, evenly spaced along the roadway; a more informal south landscape zone reflects the adjacent neighborhoods of smaller-scale hotels and single-family houses.

The Indian Wells Specific Plan captures elements of the desert within the town boundaries; reminds the town and region of its unique heritage; augments the public realm with cultural and civic amenities; and provides a realistic plan for future development.

1

2

3

1 Plein Air painting
2 Patterned Indian bowl
3 Indian well
4 Design principles diagram
5 Desert billboard

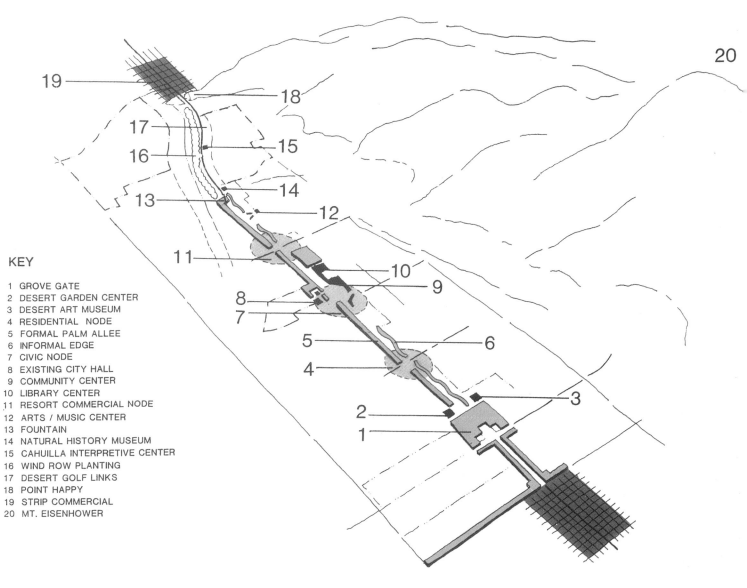

20

19
18
17
16
15
14
13
12
11
10
9
8
7
5
6
4
3
2
1

## KEY

1 GROVE GATE
2 DESERT GARDEN CENTER
3 DESERT ART MUSEUM
4 RESIDENTIAL NODE
5 FORMAL PALM ALLEE
6 INFORMAL EDGE
7 CIVIC NODE
8 EXISTING CITY HALL
9 COMMUNITY CENTER
10 LIBRARY CENTER
11 RESORT COMMERCIAL NODE
12 ARTS / MUSIC CENTER
13 FOUNTAIN
14 NATURAL HISTORY MUSEUM
15 CAHUILLA INTERPRETIVE CENTER
16 WIND ROW PLANTING
17 DESERT GOLF LINKS
18 POINT HAPPY
19 STRIP COMMERCIAL
20 MT. EISENHOWER

4

Indian Wells Specific Plan

5

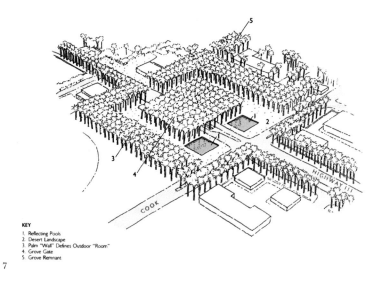

KEY
1. Reflecting Pools
2. Desert Landscape
3. Palm "Wall" Defines Outdoor "Room"
4. Grove Gate
5. Grove Remnant

7

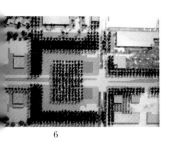

6

8

9

10

Indian Wells Specific Plan

11

12

13

14

15

Indian Wells Specific Plan

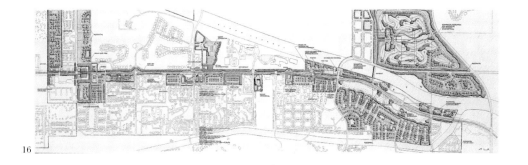

16

# Los Angeles Area Chamber of Commerce

Design/Completion 1987/1990
Los Angeles, California
Hillman Properties, Smith and Hricik Development Co.
64,000 square feet
Steel frame, precast concrete panels, granite

The Los Angeles Area Chamber of Commerce headquarters is the first new building to be implemented in the Specific Plan area of Central City West, a large, mixed-use commercial district west of the Harbor Freeway in downtown Los Angeles. The building provides a new focus for the Southern California business community and accommodates both public and private programs. As well as housing the Chamber of Commerce, the classically organized, publicly spirited building provides leasable commercial office space.

The centrally located front entry, marked by a large archway, opens onto a two-story, skylit reception lobby and the pre-function space that serves the Chamber boardroom. A monumental stair at the end of the lobby axis leads to private Chamber offices. The boardroom offers views of downtown Los Angeles across the Harbor Freeway and opens onto a small shaded garden for outdoor events.

The precast concrete and natural stone elevations are broken rhythmically by articulated bay windows. These multi-surface windows combine a range of high-performance glass surfaces and custom aluminum frames. Commissioned works of art by Billy Al Bengston and Simon Toparovsky are integrated into the public spaces.

1

2    3

4

5

6

7

Los Angeles Area
Chamber of Commerce

# 6100 Canoga Avenue

Design 1985
Woodland Hills, California
LaSalle Partners
600,000 square feet
Steel frame, precast concrete with natural stones,
multiple high-performance glasses

6100 Canoga Avenue is a state-of-the-art low-rise office campus in Southern California's Warner Center. The four office buildings and parking structure are organized along an axis, creating a project identity reminiscent of English park buildings of the 19th century. All four lobbies are accessible either from the central *parterre* garden or from the continuous perimeter arcade. The two buildings along Canoga Avenue are joined on the fifth and sixth floors, forming a four-story symbolic gateway to the project and the embroidered garden within. This bridge has the added benefit of creating large, flexible superfloors.

The building exteriors combine precast concrete, natural stone inlays, and a highly articulated glass curtainwall system. The central garden area unifies the primary plane of the project with the use of lawn panels, pathways, flowering hedgerows, and shade trees. Stone columns, patterned paving, and custom lights for evening access define the surrounding arcade.

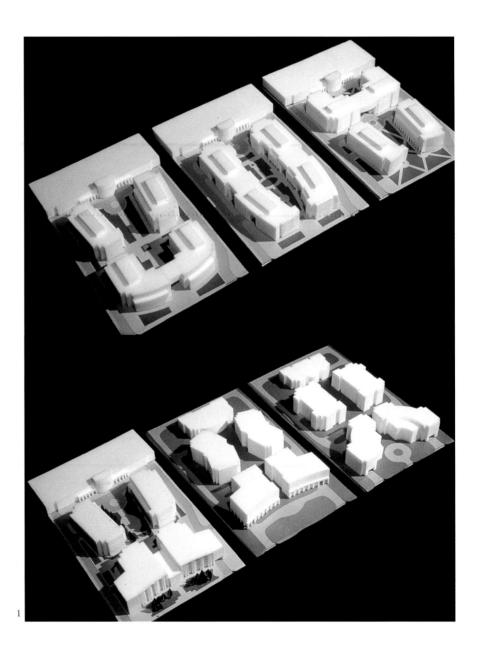

1

2

3

6100 Canoga Avenue

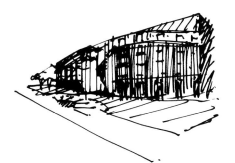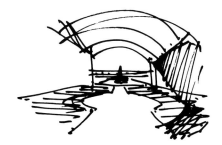

5

4

6

7

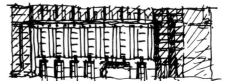

6100 Canoga Avenue

107

# William Morris Rodeo

Design/Completion 1988/1991
Beverly Hills, California
William Morris Agency
72,000 square feet
Precast concrete, granite, high-performance glass, Fior di Pesca marble

This office building for the historic William Morris talent agency is located one block south of the Rodeo Drive shopping area of Beverly Hills and abuts a quiet residential district. The detailing and metered, rhythmic facades of the building project an elegant institutional presence while complementing the scale of the adjacent domestic neighborhood.

The length of the three-story structure is broken into a series of lively smaller elements which mirror the pattern and rhythm of the intimate scale of the street. The facade is composed of rose-colored, sandblasted precast concrete, banded in rustications of Fior di Pesca marble. The tripartite window system, articulated in bronze-finished aluminum frames, creates a lively shadow pattern on the street facades. On the third floor there is a rooftop terrace for outdoor activity. The small oval lobby is finished in natural stone with a coffered plaster ceiling.

1

4

2

3

5

6

William Morris Rodeo

# Warner Bros. Office Building

Design/Completion 1991/1994
Burbank, California
270,000 square feet
Multiple glasses, EIFS exterior wall system, structural steel,
stainless steel and aluminum window wall system, natural stones

The Warner Bros. "Bridge" Office Building, on the Warner Bros. studio lot, is the first building in the studio's new master plan. To meet the requirements for large floor plates and to satisfy site density constraints, the building bridges a studio access road, creating two lobbies at ground level and a 60,000-square-foot (gross) floor plate on the second through fifth floors. The building configuration and floor plan provide the client with multiple points of access while creating additional floorspace over the street for the required large floor areas. This feature gives greater identity to individual tenants within the building and provides the flexibility necessary to accommodate future changes in the entertainment industry.

The long building is segmented to allow its mass to be perceived as a series of smaller scale elements by pedestrians. It's low profile ensures that it does not hinder filming on the adjacent lot. Window patterns vary in location, depth, and material to enrich the exterior and differentiate the accessible ground floors, the midsection, and the penthouse floor. The all-glass bridge traverses the building and creates a single circulation system within.

1

2

3

4

1  Aerial view of site model
2  West elevation of model
3  South elevation of model
4  North elevation of model
5  West entry
6  Ground floor plan

Warner Bros. Office Building

111

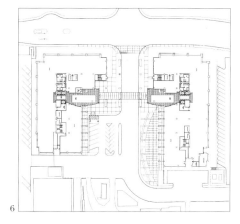

7

7  Elevator cab interior
8  Reception desk and lobby
9  Entrance and lobby
10 Early sketch of bridge concept (Scott Johnson)

8

9

Warner Bros. Office Building

10

11

Warner Bros. Office Building

## Pasadena Towers

Design/Completion 1988/1990
Pasadena, California
Ahmanson Commercial Development Company
456,000 square feet
Honed travertines, natural stones, custom ironwork,
colored and sandblasted precast concrete

This office and financial center, built for Home Savings of America, is a mixed-use development in the heart of historic Old Town, Pasadena. The project includes two nine-story office towers of 205,000 square feet each; 16,000 square feet of street level retail shops; a 30,000-square-foot three-story branch bank for Home Savings of America; and a seven-level parking structure for 1,400 cars. The project responds to strict zoning requirements and provides an anchor for Pasadena's redevelopment initiative.

Although a private project, the development is publicly spirited: pedestrian arcades and lobbies provide access through the buildings to the center of the block; circulation between parking and lobbies is weather-protected; and public areas include spirited paving and landscaping. A motor court plaza occupies the center of the project.

Interior lobbies and public spaces are highly articulated formal rooms which recall elements of historic Pasadena. Polychromed paving patterns, detailed furnishings and millwork, and artwork by Richard Haas all enhance the richness of the project in this unique location.

1  Courtyard entry
2  Site model
3  Interior arcade
4  Driveway elevation
5  Interior arcade
6  Aerial view from Colorado Boulevard
   and Lake Street

3

4

5

6

Pasadena Towers

7

8

9

10

11

12

13

Pasadena Towers

119

# Valencia Town Center Office Building

Design/Completion 1993/1996
Valencia, California
Newhall Land and Farming Company
50,000 square feet
Steel frame, EIFS exterior wall system, aluminum curtainwall,
tiles, natural flagstones

This office building inaugurates the first major building project on Town Center Drive in Valencia. The street is planned as part of an urban village, an evolving link between the area's newest regional shopping mall and the office and retail space which will bring new services to the population of Valencia.

The highly articulated facades enrich the building exterior and set a lively tone for the street. Multi-colored flagstone paving, street lights, benches, and shade trees enhance the entrance to the new building. The ground level of the structure has broad expanses of arched window glass framed by shade pergolas and flanked by trellised vines. Elevations have smooth plaster surfaces with cast-stone tiles and flagstones.

1

Valencia Town Center Office Building    121

# Queensway Bay Parking Garage

Design/Completion 1995/1997
Long Beach, California
City of Long Beach
468,000 square feet
Poured-in-place concrete, precast concrete, zinc panels

Adjacent to the Long Beach Aquarium and the Promenade, the Queensway Bay Parking Garage houses approximately 1,400 cars and provides an element of fun and excitement appropriate to its location. The project's form and maritime-themed detailing respond to the curvilinear and abstract waves of the aquarium.

The south elevation facing the aquarium has a metal paneled screen wall with cutouts in the shapes of local marine life. These cutouts act as view portals for visitors as they approach and leave the garage elevators. An abstract wave form, constructed of rolled zinc panels, marks the main vehicular entrance on Shoreline Drive.

The tall, curvilinear elevator tower at the southeast corner acts as a beacon for pedestrians returning from the Promenade. The rooftop, which acts as a staging/viewing area for the annual Long Beach Grand Prix, has an integrally colored concrete roof surface to reduce glare. A special aquatic-themed paving design and an articulated stair tower at the northwest corner soften the roofscape and provide visual interest for observers in adjacent taller buildings.

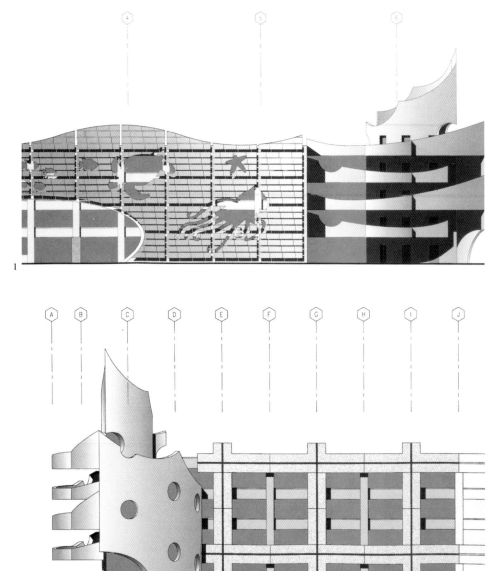

122

1    South elevation detail
2    Elevator tower
3    View from Aquarium Way
4    Plan
5    South elevation
6    Ramp elevation

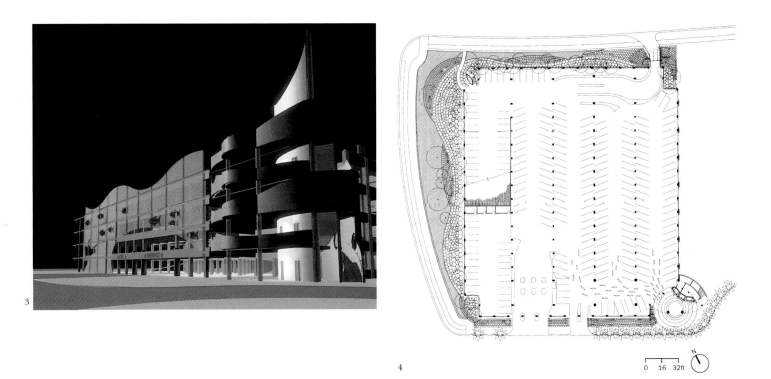

3

4

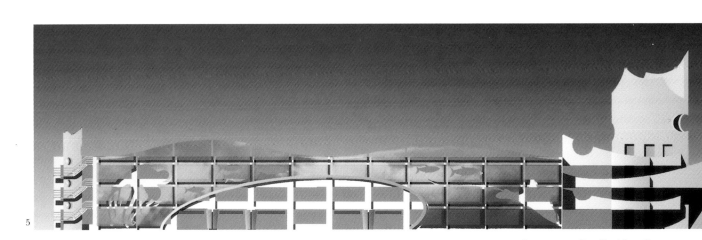

5

Queensway Bay Parking Garage                123

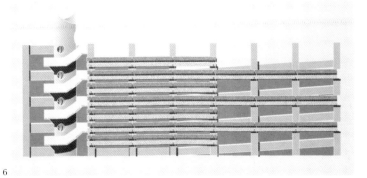

6

# University of California at Irvine "Main Street"

Design 1987
Irvine, California
University of California at Irvine, Office of Physical Planning
450,000 square feet

The University of California at Irvine "Main Street" introduces a pedestrian-oriented urban focal point into a suburban campus loosely organized around a central park. This concept for a retail street brings external services into the campus, linking it to the surrounding community. The street creates a sense of place through its density, concentration of uses, architectural scale, and massing relationships.

The plan creates a hierarchy of public spaces which integrate the street into the existing campus. Four zones provide transitional spaces and activities for the pedestrian: the urban, mixed-use Main Street; a series of landscaped semi-public courtyards; a set of academic buildings; and Aldrich Park at the center of campus.

Approximately 85,000 square feet of retail and service uses are located in infill buildings along Main Street. A plaza and a ceremonial staircase to the main library mark the midpoint of the street; an expanded student union and parking structure anchor the northwest end; and a proposed university guest house, co-op department store, and parking structure anchor the southeast end. A cross axis through the central plaza connects Aldrich Park to the university town center and encourages community access to campus facilities.

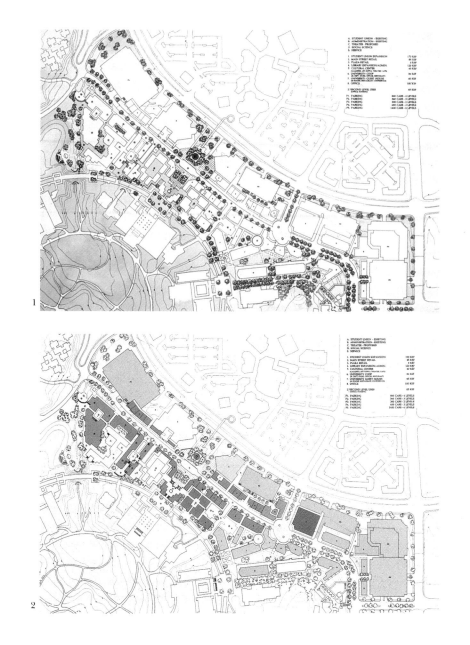

124

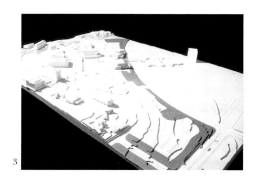

3

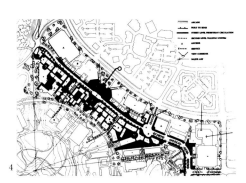

4

5

6

University of California at Irvine
"Main Street"

125

# Otis College of Art and Design

Design 1987
Los Angeles, California
Otis College of Art and Design
70,000 square feet

The Otis College of Art and Design Master Plan includes the design of new structures and the redesign and reprogramming of existing buildings at the historic downtown site. The primary design challenge was to integrate the separate parts into a single campus while providing secure points of entry into the new ensemble.

New construction along Wilshire Boulevard continues the wall of the gallery building to include a multimedia resource center. This structure steps up to a five-story studio building along Carondelet Street. The naturally lit painting and sculpture studios are connected by a wide glass gallery that provides both circulation and space for the exhibition of student work. The new construction creates a unified courtyard bordering the student lounge and media center, and centralizes circulation.

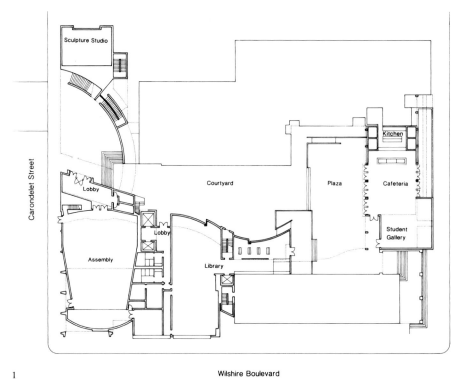

1

Wilshire Boulevard

2

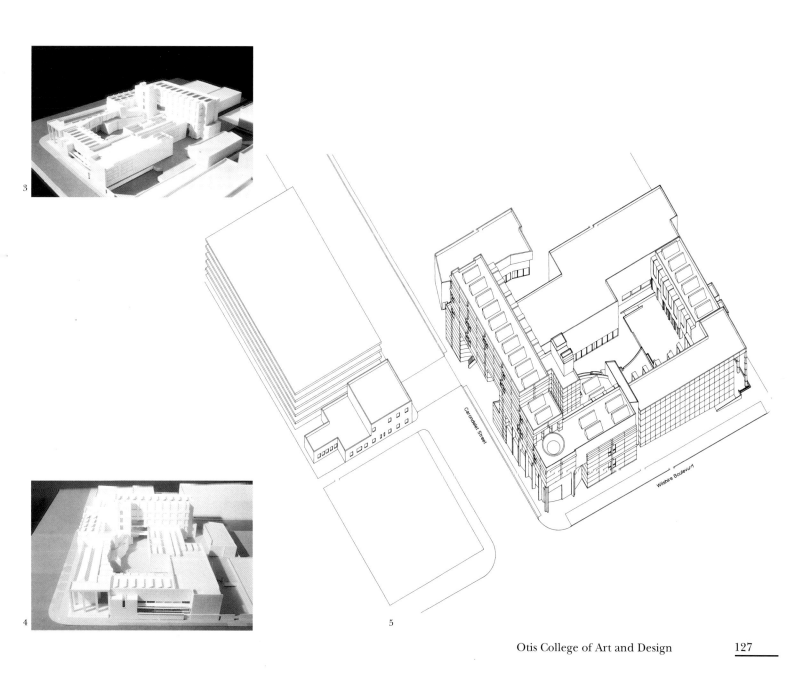

3

4

5

Otis College of Art and Design      127

6

7

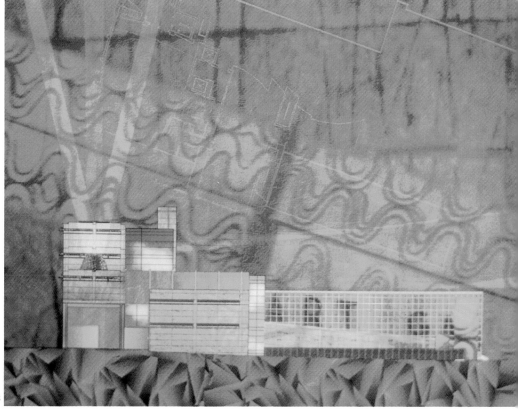

8

Otis College of Art and Design          129

9

# Marlborough School

Design/Completion 1994/1996
Los Angeles, California
20,000 square feet
Painted masonry, structural steel, aluminum and glass window wall,
steel rails, screens, canopies

The two-phase project for Marlborough School included master planning and programming for strategic upgrades, and the expansion of classroom, administrative, staff, and performing arts spaces. The design process included continuous coordination with students, faculty, staff, and administration.

The first phase includes renovation of the existing science facility to accommodate biology, physics, and chemistry laboratories, and lecture rooms. The renovation also improves office areas and other special-use spaces such as an intimate theater, a music room, dressing rooms, and a dance studio.

The new construction includes a two-story addition housing new classrooms and laboratories and an infill addition between two ground floor bays of the existing central building for admissions and college counseling.

1

2

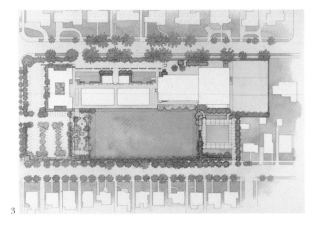

3

1  Dance studio
2  Science laboratory interior
3  Rendered site plan with proposed recreation fields
4  Science and arts wing
5  Exterior view over swimming pool

4

5

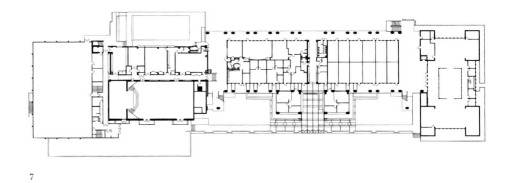

7

8

9

Marlborough School

133

10

# Shoshana Wayne Gallery

Design/Completion 1986/1987
Santa Monica, California
Shoshana and Wayne Blank
5,000 square feet
Dry wall, polished concrete floors,
sandblasted timber structure

Shoshana Wayne Gallery involved the
conversion of a former recording studio
into a painting and sculpture gallery.
The building was reconfigured to provide
exhibition space that is easily divisible
into three separate zones to accommodate
individual shows. In the rear of the
structure, painting and sculpture storage
is designed in a mobile and highly
organized frame system. At the rear of
the gallery is a large room for print and
flatwork storage and viewing.

The finishes are minimal and unadorned.
Floors are of polished sealed concrete,
the timber columns are sandblasted, and
the ceiling structure is exposed. Floating
plaster walls provide exhibition surfaces,
while selected glass panels provide
visibility between the two private offices
and the gallery.

1

134

Shoshana Wayne Gallery

# Karl Bornstein Gallery

Design/Completion 1988
Santa Monica, California
Karl Bornstein
14,000 square feet
Dry wall, polished concrete floor,
sandblasted timber structure
Custom millwork, hand-stained
brick facade

The Karl Bornstein Gallery converts
former industrial space into a new gallery
for the exhibition of contemporary art.
The building is divided into four distinct
areas: the exhibition gallery; private offices
and art storage; administrative offices for
printworks; and a preparation and
distribution area for printworks. The
exterior brick facade of the building was
stripped and sandblasted and steel frames
were added for windows, entries, and
skylights. Floating exhibition walls and
millwork are located to provide flexibility
in the installation of artwork in the gallery.

1&2

3

Karl Bornstein Gallery

135

# "Eye to Eye" Stage Set

Design/Completion 1993
Hollywood, California
Collage Dance Theatre

"Eye to Eye" was a collaboration between five Southern California choreographers (Heidi Duckler, Stephanie Gilliland, Scott Heinzerling, Katherine LaNasa, and Yaelisa) under the direction of Heidi Duckler, the artistic director of the Collage Dance Theatre, as part of the 1993 Los Angeles Philharmonic "Summer Nights" series.

Stage sets for "Eye to Eye" were created especially for the John Anson Ford Amphitheater in Hollywood, treating the performance space itself as a site-specific venue. The sets comprised a large group of bold, geometric, woven wood forms, designed to be mobile and interpretive. These elements were chosen and employed in various ways by each group of dancers in a series of five half-hour performances. The sets evoked abstract representations of the provisional landscape which describes Los Angeles.

1

"Eye to Eye" Stage Set

# SELECTED AND CURRENT WORKS III

# Byron Winery

Design/Completion 1994/1996
Santa Maria Valley, California
Byron Vineyard and Winery
32,000 square feet
Structural wood framing, arched steel trusses

A sweeping, curved roof, reminiscent of the rolling hills surrounding the site, is the primary expression of the new Byron Winery. In keeping with California's visionary tradition, the winery is both futuristic and respectful of the land from which it grows. Cedar planks, iron windows, and zinc roofing form its main components. Highlighted by free-form panels of strong earth pigments, a long, shaded portico runs the length of the building, providing entry to the tasting and barrel rooms and views of the vineyards below.

The project features 11,000 square feet of barrel aging facilities controlled for optimal humidity and temperature, and accommodates a gravity-flow wine-making process. The winery's state-of-the-art technology includes custom grape sorting tables, portable tank transports, and a unique drainage system in the fermentation cellar. Byron is situated on 640 acres of vineyards and has a current production capacity of 70,000 cases annually.

1

Byron Winery

4

Byron Winery                                    143

8

9

10

11

12

Byron Winery

# Opus One

Design/Completion 1984/1990
Oakville, California
Baroness Philippine de Rothschild and the Robert Mondavi Family
60,000 square feet
Concrete and masonry structure
Limestone, clear redwood, oak, brushed stainless steel

The Opus One winery, a joint venture between Baroness Philippine de Rothschild and the Robert Mondavi Family, is a unique collaboration between a renowned California vintner and a celebrated European winemaker. The winery is nestled inside a crescent-shaped berm and extends itself into the rural landscape. A long entry drive bisects the berm and leads to a central courtyard. Here, a semicircular arcade links together all the public functions of the winery, such as reception, entertaining, kitchens, and administrative offices.

The building's plan and section allow for a gravity-flow process of wine-making: grapes are delivered to the winery at a high elevation and are fermented and barreled lower down, so there is minimal mechanical movement of the wine. The primary benefit of the berm is that it insulates the cellars and wine-making areas on the winery's lower level. Fermentation tank rooms and grape loading and preparation areas are located at the rear. The dramatic *Grand Chai* (first-year barrel cellar), with the tasting room located at its apex, is surrounded by second-year barrel rooms, *rincoirs*, and support functions.

Native plantings and the building's natural finishes connect this grand geometric plan to the spectacular Napa Valley landscape.

1

2

1 Earth berm
2 Model
3 View from the vineyard
4 Front entry
5 Section

Opus One

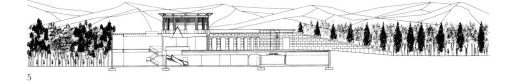

6

7

8

9

10

11

Opus One

12

13

14

15

Opus One

16

# Gallo Sonoma Estate Cellars

Design 1992
Healdsburg, California
Gallo Sonama Estate Cellars
25,000 square feet
Reinforced concrete
Natural stone, resawn oak, clear plate glass

The design for Gallo Sonoma Estate Cellars sites the winery on the northern edge of a 6,000-acre vineyard in Healdsburg, Sonoma County, California. The 25,000-square-foot winery is designed to accommodate a marketing, tasting, and visitor center for the wine and restaurant industry. The building program graciously provides for a 10,000-square-foot barrel storage area as well as a tasting room, wine library, reception hall, and kitchen; offices; and extensive outdoor patios, terraces and natural gardens.

The building is uniquely nestled into the rolling hills, deriving its design metaphors from the hills, trees, and meadows of the surrounding landscape. The building's form dissolves into the landscape through a series of curved walls and terraces that respond to the existing topography. The site plan preserves the indigenous Californian oak trees.

Reinforced concrete is the main structural material of the building; field stone, natural oak, and clear glass are used as the finish materials to visually defer to the surrounding landscape.

1

1   Photomontage
2   Roof plan view of site model
3   Site plan sketch (Scott Johnson)

2

Gallo Sonoma Estate Cellars                    153

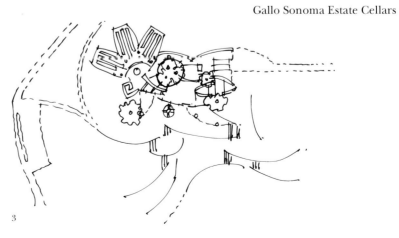

3

7

Gallo Sonoma Estate Cellars

155

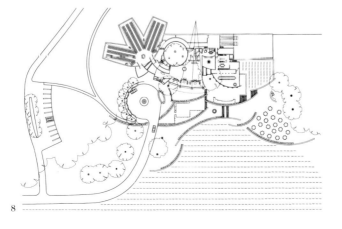

8

# Private House, St Helena

Design/Completion 1992/1994
St Helena, California
4,000 square feet
Wood frame, poured-in-place concrete foundation, stone floors,
cedar plank siding, composition roof

This house is sited on a promontory above
a hillside vineyard and looks eastward over
the Napa Valley and 60 acres of wilderness
bordering California State parkland and
Iron Mine Creek. The driveway passes
through a grove of native oaks before
joining a 200-foot-long wall that both
bisects the house beyond and forms the
basis of its plan.

The wall passes through the house
entrance and descends through a series
of stone steps and landings which follow
the contours of the hill. It steps down into
a central gallery and terminates in a living
room defined by three glass walls and two
flanking stone fireplaces. The wall defines
the house by dividing the private spaces
(bedrooms and baths) from the
communal spaces (gallery, kitchen,
dining, studio, and living area). The
longitudinal path through the house
is modulated by four glazed thresholds,
whose alternating bands of glass at floor
and ceiling give slivered views of the
landscape.

1

2

1 House sited among vines
2 Rear elevation
3 Front elevation
4 Site plan sketch (Scott Johnson)

3

Private House, St Helena

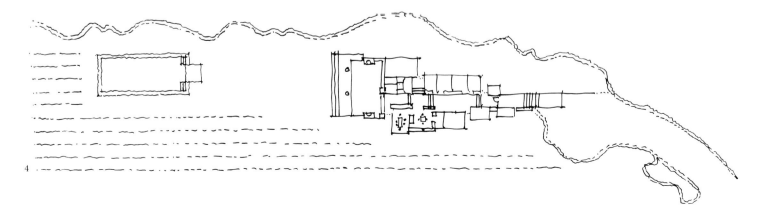

4

5

6

7

10

8&9

Private House, St Helena

Private House, St Helena                    161

# DreamWorks SKG

Design/Completion 1995/1997
Los Angeles, California
Maguire Thomas Partners/DreamWorks SKG
100-acre site

JFP prepared the overall design and master plan concepts for the new studio facilities of DreamWorks SKG as the focus of a 100-acre entertainment, media, and technology district in the new planned community of Playa Vista in Los Angeles. In contrast to the first generation of Los Angeles studios built more than 60 years ago, the DreamWorks studio places the back lot at the core of the complex.

By combining new digital technical facilities with more traditional production offices, the studio encourages creative feature film and television work in an informal indoor and outdoor setting. The development concept emphasizes the most advanced technology such as fiber optics and digital information systems, placed within a soft-edged, low-rise, heavily landscaped setting.

Three different concepts (radial, allée, serpentine) each situate 3 million square feet of buildings on 100 acres of land.

Other entertainment and technology businesses will share the studio campus with DreamWorks SKG in an atmosphere of creative collaboration.

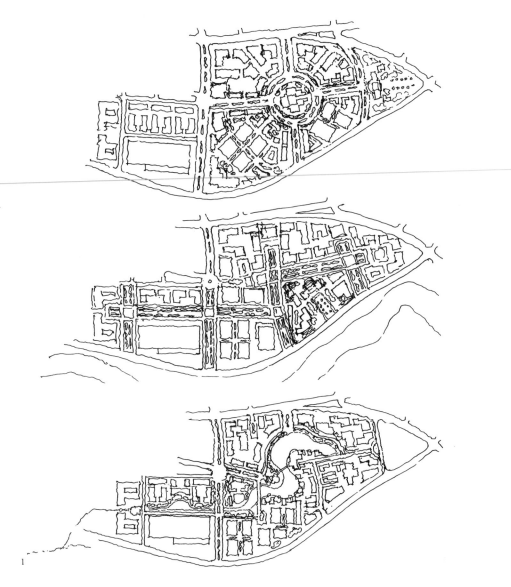

1

1   Alternative concept sketches (William Fain)
2   West view of model
3   Plan view of model
4   Digital platform

2

3

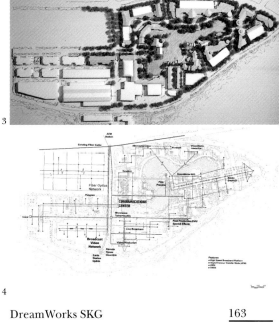

4

DreamWorks SKG                163

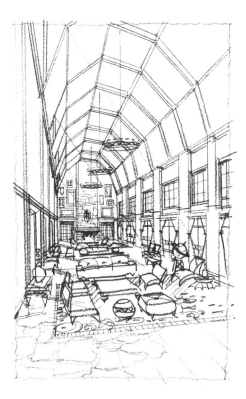

5

6

7

DreamWorks SKG

# CNS Resort

Design 1991
Talofofo, Saipan, Northern Mariana Islands
Co-You Niizeki Saipan Development
220 acres

Located on the high slopes of the northeast coast of Saipan, in the North Pacific Ocean, the CNS Resort features a 500-room hotel and golf club surrounded by an 18-hole golf course with extensive golf practice facilities, a tropical-theme water park, tennis courts, a health club with a spa and Japanese baths, retail shops, and restaurants.

The low wings of the main resort complex, designed and sited to offer dramatic views of the shoreline, are terraced to create a low profile in the luxuriant landscape. Hipped roofs with deep overhangs recall traditional Saipan and Pacific Island architecture and provide shade.

Employee housing has outdoor courtyards, a central dining area, and recreation facilities. Native *tangan-tangan* and riverine plant communities are preserved throughout the project. Access to the site is via a rural road through a limestone forest.

1

2

3

4&5

CNS Resort

6

7

8

9

CNS Resort

10

11

12

13

14

CNS Resort

## Al-Khobar Resort Hotel

Design 1995
Al-Khobar, Saudi Arabia
Al-Obiayi Contracting & Maintenance Company
125 acres

The Al-Khobar Resort, located on a 125-acre landfill arc, begins at the city's edge and culminates at the hotel tower complex. The resort includes a 350-room hotel and a business and conference center. In keeping with Saudi Arabian custom, a full range of health club and recreation opportunities provides separate facilities for men and families. Luxury villas, featuring individual boat docks and beaches, are located along the arc and on separate islands for a completely private environment.

In the preliminary phase of this project, three distinctly different schemes were developed: the courtyard, the sail, and the lighthouse tower. The lighthouse tower was developed for further study. The multi-faceted hotel tower offers standard and double rooms and executive suites. The top of the spiraling ziggurat-capped tower contains private luxury suites, a royal suite, a restaurant, and a panoramic view lounge. Dramatic exterior lighting of the upper levels completes the "lighthouse beacon" resort theme.

The resort is linked to the city by a complex of public recreational and commercial facilities, including a public marina, a retail galleria with ice rink, an amphitheater and IMAX theater, a historical museum, and an aquarium.

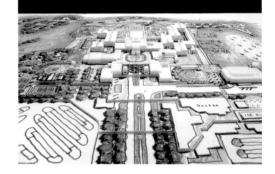

1

172

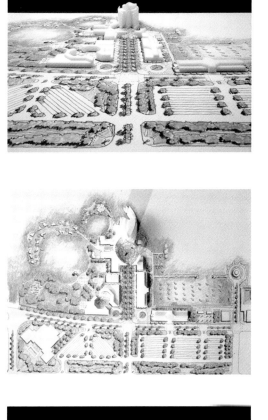

2

3

Al-Khobar Resort Hotel

4

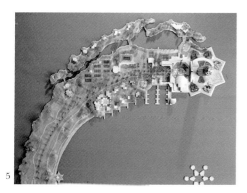

5

6

7

8

Al-Khobar Resort Hotel

175

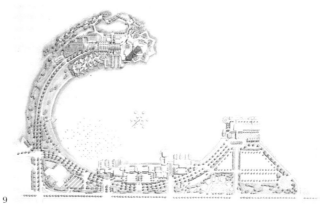

9

# LeoPalace Resort

Design/Completion 1988/1993
Yona Municipality, Guam
Miyama Development International, Tokyo
1,300 acres

JFP was commissioned to master plan and design this $1.5 billion resort on the island of Guam in the Mariana Islands in the Western Pacific Basin. The project's 1,300-acre site, approximately 2 per cent of the island area, contains 3,000 housing units and a wide range of recreational facilities, including 45 holes of golf designed by Jack Nicklaus and Arnold Palmer. Retail, amenities, and a 200-room luxury hotel cluster around an 8-acre lake to form the village center.

Natural beauty and environmental sensitivity, along with Spanish colonial history and ancient archaeology, were all important factors in the design of the LeoPalace Resort. The master plan captures the site's sweeping views of both the Philippine Sea and the Pacific Ocean. Existing wetlands, streams, and lakes were preserved and incorporated into the enhanced landscape. New buildings were designed as modern variations on the 400-year-old Spanish heritage, executed in masonry and tile both to withstand Pacific typhoons and to harmonize with indigenous materials and craftsmanship. Six latte stone building sites, characteristic of prehistoric building in the Mariana Islands, were discovered during the planning process and were identified for restoration with contemporaneous artifacts dedicated to an on-site museum.

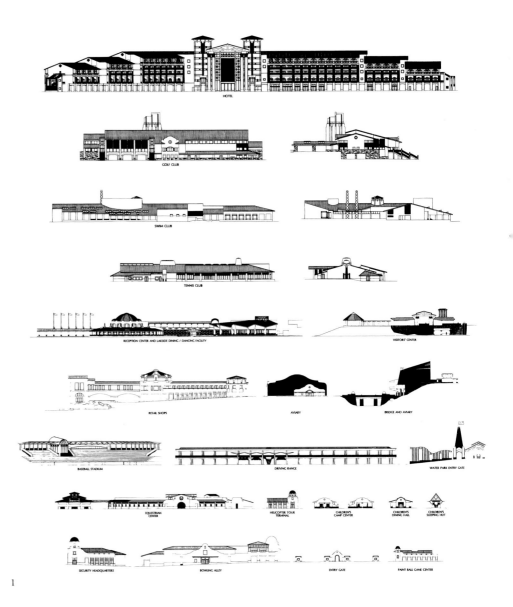

1

1 Public building elevations
2 Village model
3 Village site plan
4 Computer model of hotel lobby

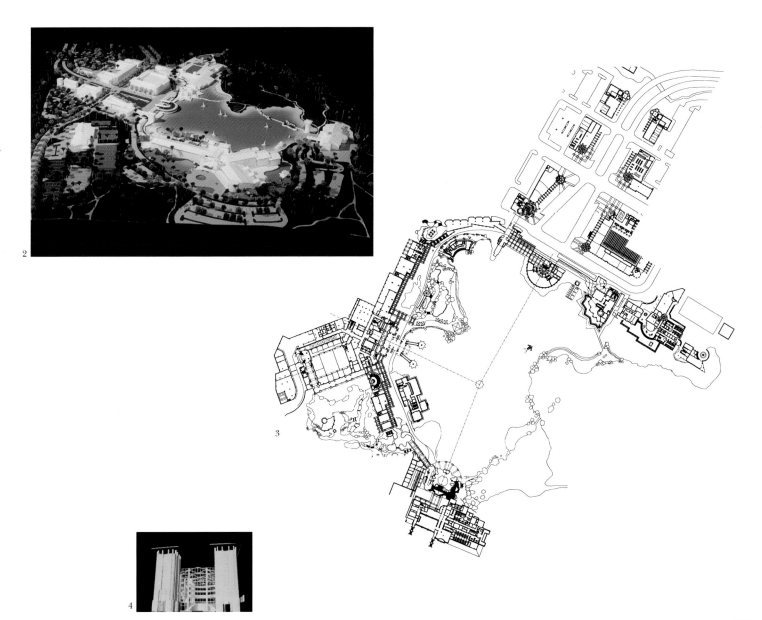

LeoPalace Resort

177

5

6

7

5  Fairway duplex housing
6  Overview of fairway with native landscape
7  Entry to golf clubhouse
8  View to eight-story condominium from pool
9  View to resort hotel from the lake
10  Entry gate
11  View to golf clubhouse from the lake

8&9

0&11

LeoPalace Resort

12

13

14

15

LeoPalace Resort

# SELECTED AND CURRENT WORKS IV

# SunAmerica Inc. Corporate Headquarters

Design/Completion 1992/1993
Los Angeles, California
76,000 square feet

This office interior, designed for the
financial services headquarters of
SunAmerica, occupies four floors of
1999 Avenue of the Stars in Century City,
California. The total office space of 76,000
square feet consists of operational and
executive floors. On the executive floors,
private offices line the radial perimeter.
This design gives each office a unique
view and provides visual interest and
drama on the interior longitudinal
corridors. Common facilities are highly
accessible around the elevator core,
with transparent conference rooms
underscoring the open, accessible nature
of the company.

The use of light and application of golden
finishes reinforces the sensibility and
imagery of SunAmerica. Interior materials
include limestone, white marble, brushed
stainless steel, and brass. Selected public
areas within the office suite are light and
minimal in character to defer to the
company's internationally recognized art
collection and the highly refined interior
details.

1

SunAmerica Inc. Corporate
Headquarters

185

6

7

8

SunAmerica Inc. Corporate
Headquarters

9

10

11

SunAmerica Inc. Corporate
Headquarters

# Warner Bros. Technical Operations

Design/Completion 1994/1995
Burbank, California
25,000 square feet
Anegre, patterned glass, textile wall panels, slate,
polished stainless steel

The interior design for the newly consolidated divisions of Warner Bros. Technical Operations includes private and executive offices, open area workstations, a screening room, a recording booth, multi-use conference rooms, and a public reception area.

Johnson Fain Partners worked closely with Warner Bros. to develop office plans and furniture selections that will serve as the design standard for all future tenant improvements.

The design creatively re-uses existing spaces and adds new interior finishes, furnishings, and equipment as well as a computer network, a fiber optics network, and state-of-the-art telecommunications. The interior finishes include light maple and anegre veneers, geometric carpet in strong natural tones, and bold fabrics and wall coverings against a neutral background.

1

1 Reception area
2 Executive office
3 Open office area

Warner Bros. Technical Operations

# Paradise Restaurant

Design/Completion 1986/1988
Torrance, California
Andrex Development Company
8,900 square feet
Steel frame, glue-laminated beams, aluminum shed siding

Paradise Restaurant is a gathering place that reflects the Pacific influence in industrial South Los Angeles. The restaurant, located at the intersection of the two busiest freeways in Los Angeles, provides a welcome alternative to standard roadside dining. This eclectic eatery has a geometric shed-style exterior with a bold white corrugated shell, an asymmetrical green metal trapezoidal roof, and circular porthole windows. The art-filled interior features custom furnishings, fabrics, and patterns from nature, and high ceilings for a feeling of openness and dramatic volume. The space is enlivened by natural light from large skylights.

An open working kitchen is in full view, and is accented with bright tiles, rotisseries, and wood-burning pizza ovens. Artist Eve Ohman created large panels of lush Pacific scenes which are suspended over the bar, kitchen, and dining areas. Custom palm-motif chairs, artifacts from the Pacific, and surfboard sinks in the lavatories are some of the elements brought together to create a Pacific setting that is both modern and informal.

1

1 Main dining room
2 Exterior view
3 Bar
4 Floor plan

2

3

Paradise Restaurant

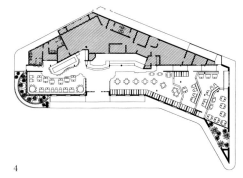
4

5

6

Paradise Restaurant                                      195

# Pircher House

Design/Completion 1989/1991
Los Angeles, California
5,000 square feet
Plaster, sandblasted Douglas fir, rosewood, sapele,
maple floors, glass tiles

This project involved a substantial
remodeling of a house in Cheviot Hills,
West Los Angeles, a neighborhood of
traditional homes. The house was
designed to accommodate the couple's
preference for entertaining in the home
and garden, and to create a showcase
for their collection of European
decorative arts.

The design significantly opens up the floor
plan of the public rooms, improving both
circulation and natural lighting to the
rooms. The display of decorative objects
and fine printwork, together with the use
of consistent finishes, unify the public
spaces and encourage movement through
the house.

The palette of finishes is generally light
and natural to provide a neutral backdrop
for artwork, with strategic placement of
color for effect. Narrow steel-framed
windows maximize daylight, while custom-
designed furniture and millwork in maple,
anegre, cherry, and rosewood provide
form in an informal setting.

1

1 Dining room
2 Study
3 Living room
4 Ground floor plan

2

3

Pircher House

4

6

7

8

Pircher House                                    199

# Warner Bros. Telepictures

Design/Completion 1993/1994
Burbank, California
8,000 square feet
Pearwood panels, stainless steel, ebonized details

The office headquarters for Warner Bros. Telepictures Productions is located adjacent to the Warner Bros. studio lot. This corporate interior space has an unusually large number of unique private offices for producers and vice presidents, as well as support staff workstations and an efficient open plan for accounting staff.

Accent materials such as pearwood panels and colorful silk fabric wall panels provide areas of focus in the sophisticated yet economical work environment. High-quality natural finishes are used in the lobby for a distinctively warm but professional environment. Standard workstations are customized to meet the needs of a range of support staff.

1

1 Open office area
2 Reception lobby
3 Floor plan

# Allied Communications Inc.

Design/Completion 1991/1992
Los Angeles, California
Allied Communications Inc.
8,500 square feet

Allied Communications Inc. is a modern, functional office interior. The office design maximizes access and contact between staff by opening up circulation space and strategically locating the private offices. Glass partitions, refined millwork, and exhibition track lighting give the space an informal tone and create a highly flexible work environment. The executives' private offices provide a neutral environment for an eclectic mix of furnishings and accessories.

4

Allied Communications Inc.

# Johnson Fain Partners Office

Design/Completion 1996/1997
Los Angeles, California
14,000 square feet
Sanded plywood, hand-trowelled plaster, domestic white marble,
panelized wall coverings

The new office for Johnson Fain Partners is a highly flexible studio environment located on the second floor of a historic International Style building in downtown Los Angeles. The design takes advantage of the 25-foot ceilings and floor-to-ceiling windows to accentuate the high level of natural light while maximizing open circulation space.

Most of the floorspace is designed as flexible open studio space with low partitions and fully networked computer workstations. Partners' offices are sheathed in sanded plywood within the overall studio volume and have oversized sliding doors which provide direct access to the open studio. Conference rooms, administrative offices, archives, and model shops are enclosed for visual and acoustic privacy.

1

2

1 Reception area
2 Partners' offices
3 Small conference room
4 Elevator lobby and reception desk
5 Studio
6 Floor plan

Johnson Fain Partners Office

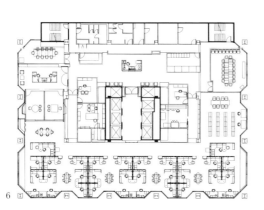

# Pacific Corporate Towers

Design/Completion 1994/1996
El Segundo, California
GE Capital Investment Advisors, CB Commercial Real Estate Group Inc.
1.6 million square feet

Built during the 1970s, Pacific Corporate Towers is a three-tower complex with 1.6 million square feet of office space. Twenty-five years after its original design, a comprehensive program of strategic upgrades and renovations updates the complex and adapts it to the current multi-tenant premium market. The project improvements include new architecture, landscaping, lighting, and environmental graphics.

The stainless steel and ceramic fritted glass signage uses silk-screened natural imagery to allude to the landscaped areas within the site. Similar imagery appears on the architectural elements spanning the entry driveway, which overhang the pedestrian walkways connecting the parking garage to the office building.

The lobby of the central office tower was redesigned to create a focus and to facilitate access through the site from building to building. The new geometry of the lobby allows diagonal circulation around a circular wall which incorporates dark wood veneers, Georgia marbles, and stainless steel detailing and hardware.

An existing triangular courtyard area, positioned between the parking structure and two of the office towers, is enclosed on the western side with a transparent "windwall" of sloped glass. The windwall helps to define the courtyard space and creates a large exterior room that acts as a landscaped oasis.

1

1 Windscreen pedestrian bridge
2 Courtyard
3 Garage entry
4 Courtyard garden
5 Courtyard at night

Pacific Corporate Towers

207

6

7

8

12

9

10

11

Pacific Corporate Towers

## 10880 Wilshire at Westwood

Design/Completion 1990/1992
Los Angeles, California
Hines Interests Limited
26,000 square feet
Limestone, custom-patterned glass and woodwork,
integrally colored concrete and anodized aluminum

This project renovated and modernized a 20-year-old, 24-story commercial office tower at the southeast corner of Westwood and Wilshire Boulevards in Westwood Village. The renovation upgraded the primary public spaces including building entrances, main lobbies, an interior retail concourse, parking and garage lobbies, and newly landscaped garden areas and exterior plazas, and improved general lighting.

Public spaces were unified with the use of new interior finishes such as granite, limestone, custom-patterned glass and woodwork, integrally colored concrete and anodized aluminum. The retail concourse was repaved in limestone, quartzite and marble, with integrated planters and seating. The building received new elevator, HVAC, and life-safety systems, and was upgraded to conform to the *Americans with Disabilites Act* (ADA), and Title 24, a state-mandated energy conservation regulation.

A new pedestrian entry with a glass and steel windwall marks the Westwood and Wilshire corner as the primary focal point of the project, and provides a hallmark entrance visible from all sides of this busy intersection.

1

10880 Wilshire at Westwood

# Union Bank Plaza

Design/Completion 1991/1994
Los Angeles, California
Equitable NLI
20,000 square feet
French limestone, stainless steel, anegre, custom millwork

Union Bank, the first high-rise tower in downtown Los Angeles, is a landmark gateway to the precinct. This substantial renovation included upgrading public areas and circulation systems throughout the building and improving Union Bank Plaza.

The design increases ground level visibility and access to the tower lobby; completely renovates the lobby, elevator vestibules, elevator cabs, and multi tenant common space; and integrates outdoor plazas and retail elements with the building's circulation systems. The renovation also fulfills new building code requirements, including the *Americans with Disabilities Act* (ADA) and Title 24, a state-mandated energy conservation regulation. The resulting transformation strengthened the overall project identity of Union Bank Plaza in the downtown landscape.

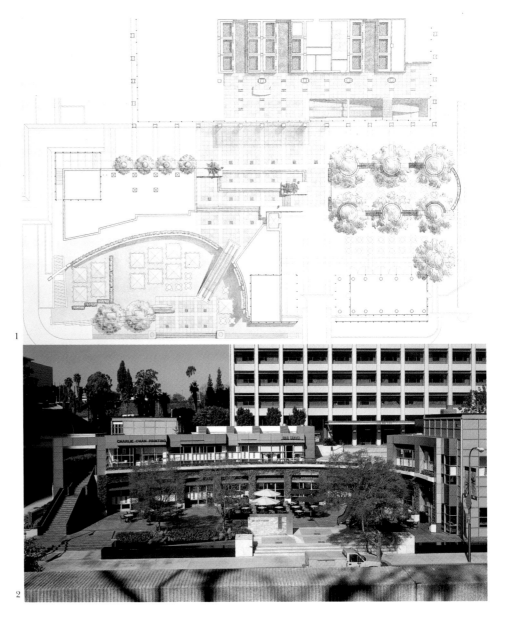

1

2

3

Union Bank Plaza

## Pacific Center

Design/Completion 1991/1992
Los Angeles, California
Pactel Properties, Cushman and Wakefield
50,000 square feet

The restoration and selective remodeling of Pacific Center, a historically significant building designed by Parkinson and Parkinson dating from 1908–1926, encompasses approximately 50,000 square feet of public area. The owners of the building determined that both functional and visual upgrading were required in order to meet contemporary standards of quality and comfort while honoring the building's status as a historic landmark.

Areas of redesign include new interior and exterior retail storefronts, standards for tenants' common space on upper floors, new lobby areas and elevator cabs, new automobile arrival, signage, and lighting.

Restoration work focuses on preserving the historically significant Beaux Arts main lobby, historic retail storefronts, architectural stone and bronze work, building directories, plaster ceilings, and marble flooring. Long-term goals involve the restoration of exterior terra cotta and other significant architectural detail.

1  Vehicle arrival
2  Building facade
3  Storefront entry
4  Ancillary corridor
5  Elevator cab interior
6  Elevator lobby

4

5

6

Pacific Center

# All Saints' Parish

Design/Completion 1994/1996
Beverly Hills, California
All Saints' Parish
17,000 square feet
Oak millwork, French limestone paving, custom iron light fixtures
and chancel accessories

The renovation and restoration of All Saints' Parish includes initial architectural improvements to the main church building and its immediate grounds and a long-term master plan for updating the main church, sanctuary, and other parish buildings. The design updates specific liturgical functions, integrates musical elements more fully into the historic building, and improves lighting throughout. It also includes the design and restoration of furnishings and millwork consistent with existing details of the 1929 landmark building designed by Roland Coate, Sr.

The design of the chancel resulted in a new, historically compatible barrel vault in the ceiling and a circular coffered wainscot at the apse to improve the transmission of music throughout the length of the nave. The chancel floor, including ambo, altar, and choir, was lowered and broadened to increase flexibility for musical programs and improve access by the congregation.

1

1  View to chancel from side aisle
2  Entry to church
3  Parish plan
4  Longitudinal building section
5  Chancel

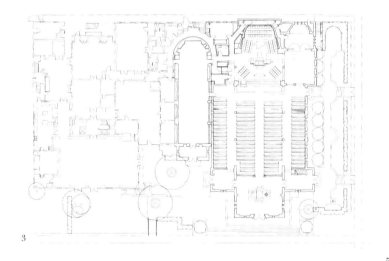

All Saints' Parish

217

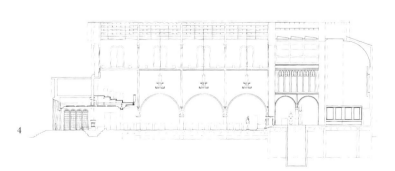

# FIRM PROFILE

With the publication of this monograph, Johnson Fain Partners marks its tenth anniversary as a design studio practicing architecture, urban design and planning, and interior design. The firm, led by Scott Johnson and William Fain, emerged from the historic office of William L. Pereira Associates and directs its creative energy toward the innovative design of a range of built structures and communities. Acknowledging the complexities of the urban landscape worldwide, Johnson Fain Partners finds unique opportunities in each project to design and detail signature environments.

The work of Johnson Fain Partners first garnered accolades 10 years ago with the dramatic success of Fox Plaza, the high-rise headquarters of 20th Century Fox Film Corporation in West Los Angeles, and the urban design plan for Hawaii's secondary urban center, the new city of Kapolei.

Fox Plaza is critically acclaimed for its immaculate detailing, exceptional silhouette, unusual siting, and its outstanding financial success as a commercial building. Kapolei represents a monumental effort to master plan an expansion community west of Honolulu, redirecting urban growth away from the significant watershed and agricultural lands of central Oahu. The low rise, residentially based design evolved from the archaeological history of the island of Oahu and creates an elegant, tropical environment sensitive to the locale.

Johnson Fain Partners draws on the strengths of a fully integrated architecture and planning practice, designing important buildings and their interiors, as well as new communities and major master plans worldwide.

# Biographies

## Scott Johnson, FAIA

Registered Architect, State of California, State of New York, Territory of Guam, and the Commonwealth of the Northern Mariana Islands
Member, National Council of Architectural Registration Board (NCARB)
Fellow, American Institute of Architects

**1987 to present**
Design Partner, Johnson Fain Partners, Los Angeles, California (formerly Johnson Fain and Pereira Associates).

**1983–87**
Design Partner, Pereira Associates, Los Angeles, California.

**1978–83**
Design Associate, Philip Johnson and John Burgee, Architects, New York, New York. Projects included:
Dade County Cultural Center, Miami, Florida
33 Maiden Lane, New York, New York
Republic Bank Center, Houston, Texas
Transco Tower, Houston, Texas
Sugarlakes Center, Houston, Texas
International Place at Fort Hill Square, Boston, Massachusetts
101 California Street, San Francisco, California
885 Third Avenue, New York, New York
Times Square Renewal Project, New York, New York

**1981**
Assistant to Arthur Drexler, Museum of Modern Art, "Three Buildings" exhibition, New York, New York.

**1975–78**
Senior Design Architect, Skidmore, Owings, and Merrill, San Francisco and Los Angeles, California. Projects included:
MCA World Headquarters, Universal City, California
Westin Hotel and South Coast Plaza, Costa Mesa, California
Harrah's Auto Museum and Hotel, Reno, Nevada

**1976–77**
Instructor, Design of Lighting Systems, Southern California Institute of Architecture, Los Angeles, California.

**1975**
The Architects' Collaborative (TAC), Cambridge, Massachusetts.

**Qualifications**
MArch, Graduate School of Design, Harvard University, 1975
AIA National Scholarship Award
Thesis: "Gestalt Theories of Perception: Ordering Systems for Lighting Architectural Space"
AB in Architecture, College of Environmental Design, University of California, Berkeley, 1972
Stanford University, Palo Alto, California, 1969–1970; Stanford University in Italy, Florence, Italy, 1970–1971

**Memberships and Lectures**
Visiting lecturer: UCLA Graduate School of Architecture and Urban Planning; UCLA Extension; USC School of Architecture; Southern California Institute of Architecture (SCI-Arc); New School of Architecture, San Diego
Executive Committee, Guild Board, USC School of Architecture
Founder, Museum of Contemporary Art (MOCA), Los Angeles
Director, Collage Dance Theatre
Member, National Council of Architectural Registration Board (NCARB)
Member, Museum of Architecture Committee, The Chicago Athenaeum
Member, National Trust for Historic Preservation
Member, Los Angeles Conservancy
Member, UCLA Dean's Council, UCLA Graduate School of Architecture and Urban Planning
Member, The Restoration Associates of the Freeman House, Hollywood California
Member, Westside Urban Forum, Los Angeles
Member, Executive Committee, Urban Land Institute
Member, Los Angeles Forum for Architecture and Urban Design
Member, Architecture and Urban Design Council, Museum of Contemporary Art (MOCA)
Cabinet Member, Real Estate/Construction Committee, Music Center Unified Fund
Chair, American Institute of Architecture, Los Angeles Chapter Design Awards
Chair, Boy Scouts of America, Construction Industry Good Scout of the Year Award Committee

# William H. Fain, Jr, FAIA

Registered Architect, State of California, Territory of Guam, and the Commonwealth of the Northern Mariana Islands
Member, National Council of Architectural Registration Board (NCARB)
Fellow, American Institute of Architects

**1987 to present**
Managing Partner and Director of Urban Design and Planning, Johnson Fain Partners, Los Angeles, California (formerly Johnson Fain and Pereira Associates).

**1980–1987**
Director of Urban Design, Pereira Associates, Los Angeles, California.

**1978–79**
Fellow, National Endowment for the Arts, Washington DC, Study of Urban Design and Zoning/Property Tax Policies.

**1976–80**
Senior Architect and Urban Designer, New Community Development Corporation, Washington, DC. Projects included:
Restructuring of the Title VII New Communities
Initiation of the Neighborhood Self-Help Development Program

**1976–77**
Visiting Lecturer and Instructor, Graduate School of Design, Harvard University.

**1975**
Consulting Urban Designer, City of Richmond, Virginia. Downtown Plan (in collaboration with Weiming Lu, Marty Millspaugh, and George Kostrisky).

**1973–75**
Senior Architect and Urban Designer, Boston Redevelopment Authority. Projects included:
Downtown Plan and site development projects
Proposal for the Tremont Street Special District (winner of *Progressive Architecture* Award 1976).

**1972–73**
Fellow, National Endowment for the Humanities (London). Study of British and French new towns (published in *Architectural Record*, December 1973).

**1970–72**
Urban Designer, Office of Midtown Planning and Development, Office of the Mayor, New York (under Jacquelin T. Robertson). Projects included:
Fifth Avenue Special Zoning District
Times Square Theater District
Madison Avenue Mall
Westside Spine
New York City Convention Center

**1968–70**
Designer, MacKinley/Winnacker Architects, Orida, California. Projects included:
Multi-family residential projects
Private residences

## Qualifications

MAUD, Graduate School of Design, Harvard University, 1975
BArch, University of California, Berkeley, 1968
Certificate, Urban and Social Planning, University of Manchester, England, 1970

## Memberships and Lectures

Chair, National AIA Regional and Urban Design Committee
Chair, National AIA Urban Design Awards Program
Past Chair, AIA Urban Design Committee
Past Chair, Transportation Committee, LA AIA
Past President, Architecture and Design Council, Museum of Contemporary Art (MOCA), Los Angeles
Past Treasurer, AIA, Los Angeles Chapter
Founders Circle, Los Angeles Music Center
Founder, Museum of Contemporary Art (MOCA), Los Angeles
Faculty Member, Southern California Institute of Architecture (SCI-Arc)
Member, Southern California Institute of Architecture (SCI-Arc) Board of Directors
Member, Marlborough School Board of Directors
Member, New Los Angeles Marketing Partnership
Member, Board of Visitors, Claremont University Graduate Humanities Center
Member, Urban Land Institute
Member, Los Angeles Area Chamber of Commerce
Member, AIA Historic Preservation Committee
Past Member, Los Angeles Library Association Board of Directors
Past Member, California Council AIA
Blue Hill Troupe, New York
Fellow, Institute of Urban Design, New York
Past Board Member, St Joseph's Foundation
Member, Los Angeles Conservancy

# Associate Partners

**Larry R. Ball, Architect,** AIA
Senior Project Manager

Mr Ball has more than 25 years of experience in all aspects of architecture, from inception through project completion, and has been responsible for a wide range of domestic and international projects. His primary responsibilities include managing the overseas office in Guam and a variety of projects in California. Mr Ball was Project Manager for Pasadena Towers, the Broadway State Office Building, and the LeoPalace Resort.

> Registered Architect, California, 1981; Michigan, 1977; Territory of Guam, 1992
>
> MArch, University of Detroit, 1975
>
> BArch (Environmental Studies), University of Detroit, 1973

**Mark R. Gershen**
Senior Planner

Mr Gershen has more than 25 years of professional experience in planning and project management. He is a specialist in environmental assessment, facilities programming, public process, quantitative aspects of master planning, technical writing, and contractual affairs. Mr Gershen was Project Manager for the Superconducting Super Collider, the Indian Wells Specific Plan, and the City of Kapolei.

> Certificate in Environmental Planning, University of California, Irvine, 1977
>
> BArch, Southern California Institute of Architecture, 1976
>
> MA, University of California, Los Angeles, 1968
>
> BA, University of California, Berkeley, 1966

**Daniel J. Janotta, Architect,** AIA
Senior Design Architect

Mr Janotta has more than 20 years of professional experience in the design of a wide range of complex institutional projects. He coordinates the application of CAD with the creative aspects of design and planning. Mr Janotta was Senior Designer for Nestlé USA Inc. Headquarters, the Warner Bros. Office Building, and 6100 Canoga Avenue.

> Registered Architect, California, 1990; Texas, 1983
>
> MArch, University of Illinois, 1980
>
> BArch, University of Illinois, 1978

# Associates

**Jeffrey Averill, Architect, AIA**
Senior Design Architect

Mr Averill has more than 20 years of professional design experience on a variety of project types, from preliminary design through construction. He has extensive experience in renovation and adaptive reuse projects and coordinates the work of various consultants. He supervised the architectural improvements to Union Bank Plaza, Marlborough School, All Saints' Parish, and the Amgen Corporate Headquarters.

    Registered Architect, California, 1983

    MArch, University of California, Berkeley, 1982

    BArch, Rice University, 1979

**Juan Carlos Begazo, Architect, AIA**
Senior Urban Designer

Mr Begazo has more than 15 years of professional experience, with a multi-disciplinary background in architecture and urban design. He has significant expertise in the design of various building types as well as the design and planning of complex, large-scale urban design projects. He participated in the award-winning designs of UCI "Main Street" and the City of Kapolei, and in the design of the Valencia Town Center buildings, and the Mission Bay Master Plan.

    Registered Architect, California, 1990

    MArch, University of California, Los Angeles, 1985

    BArch, California Polytechnic University, San Luis Obispo, 1983

**Stephen E. Levine, Architect, AIA**
Senior Urban Designer

Mr Levine has a multi-disciplinary background in architecture, landscape architecture, planning, and urban design. He has more than 25 years of experience in the design and management of a variety of master planning assignments, including resorts, multi-use complexes, corporate and civic centers, transit malls, and waterfront developments. Mr Levine worked on the master plans for LeoPalace Resort, Mission Bay, and Amgen.

    Registered Architect, California, 1987

    MArch, University of Pennsylvania, 1971

    BArch, University of Pennsylvania, 1968

**Robert P. Shaffer, Architect,** AIA
Senior Planner

Mr Shaffer is an urban designer with more than
30 years of experience in the USA and overseas.
He specializes in land-use plans and in the
preparation of airport and transportation design
studies and environmental impact studies.
Mr Shaffer worked on the Los Angeles Civic Center
Enhancement Plan, Amgen Master Plan, Norton
Air Force Base re-use plan, and NAS Agana
in Guam.

> Registered Architect, California, 1974
>
> BArch, Renssalaer Polytechnic Institute, 1965
>
> BS (Building Science), Renssalaer Polytechnic
> Institute, 1965

**Riccardo Tossani, Architect,** RAIA
Senior Urban Designer

Mr Tossani has more than 15 years of international
professional experience in the planning and design
of large-scale complex facilities. He specializes in
urban infrastructure and renewal and brings a multi-
disciplinary approach to urban design projects. Mr
Tossani supervised the LeoPalace Resort project in
Guam, and worked on Sunflower City, Bangkok, and
Trump Wilshire Center.

> Registered Architect, Australia, 1981
>
> MArch (Urban Design), Harvard Graduate
> School of Design, 1988
>
> Certificate in Urban Transport Planning and
> Analysis, University of Florence, Italy, 1985
>
> BArch (Hons), University of Adelaide, Adelaide,
> Australia, 1980

**Mark W. Zwagerman, Architect,** AIA
Senior Project Manager

Mr Zwagerman has more than 10 years of professional experience in the design and implementation of renovations, interiors, and new construction. His responsibilities include project management, design development, production supervision, construction phase coordination, and contract administration. He worked on the Amgen Corporate Headquarters, Byron Winery, Fox Plaza, and several interiors projects for Warner Bros.

Registered Architect, California, 1996

BFA Concentration in Interior Design, Colorado State University, 1987

# Collaborators

Brian Aamoth
Rodolfo Abrio
Kimberly Aikman
William Akiyama
Yvonne Alexander
Margot Alofsin
David Alpaugh
Eric Altizer
Farooq Ameen
Magda Andreos

Sherri Armstrong
Lauri Arneson
Romeo Asprec
Richard Auton
Jeffrey Avrill

Alireza Badie
Amy Bailey
Christian Baker

Maria Baldenegro
Larry Ball
Ali Barar
Juan Carlos Begazo
Dolores Bell
Jason Bell
Neil Birnbrauer
Daniel Blander
Robin Bloch
Diana Bohan
Demetrio Boo
Karen Boysen
Louis Bretana
Betty Burks
Aurora Bustamante

Carlito Calabia
Elizabeth Camayo
Ronald Cannan
Leah Carron
Barbara Cass
Lisa Castro
Henry Chaikin
Christina Chan
Jonathan Chang
Quin-Cheng Chen
Warren Chen
Judy Cheng

Vartan Cialichian
Janet Clifton
Kim Colin
Charles Cordero
Andrew Cox
Jerry Craig
John Crandell
Caleb Crawford
Charles Crawford
Chris Crolle
Joseph Cruz
Oscar de la Cruz
Matthew Cummings
Victor Cusack

John Danielian
Patric Dawe
David Decker
Pearl Diggs
Jay Dimaggio

Lori East
Brenda Economides
Edmund Einy
Carmen Epstein
Jonathan Evans
Ronald Evitts

William Fain
Davood Fakharian
Janice Faucett
Heidi Fichtenbaum
Clarence Fields
Joshua Fine
Carol Fisher
Irene Frankel
Sheri Frim
John Frost
Bruce Fullerton
Brent Fuqua
Marc Futterman

Mark Gajda
Arthur Garcia
Christ Garness
Mark Gershen
Brent Gesell
David Gevers
Leo Gomez
Kevin Gray
Richard Greenberg
Nina Gregory
Charles Grein
Jennifer Gridley
Steve Grippentrog

Roddy Hames
Sherry Hammond
Stephen Hanover
Mark Hembree
Lisa Hill
John Hillbrand
Maricela Hinojosa
Megumi Hironaka
Michele Hoye
Linda Hoyt
James Hsu
David Huang
Marlin Hutchison

Nina Ifurung
Laura Intscher
Jennifer Iselin
Atsuko Itoda

Craig Jameson
Dan Janotta
Scott Johnson

Barbara Kaplan
Bette Kennedy
Mark Kim

# Collaborators continued

Tricia Knopf
Michael Knopoff
Norman Kondy
Jacques Kravtchenko
Neil Kritzinger
Jerry Kuriyama
Kurtis Kusumoto
Daniel Kwok

Renato Lacson
Janie Huoy-Jen Lai
Roberta Lawry
Alistair Laws
Robert Lawson
Loretta Lee
Benjamin Levin
Fernand Levin
Ben Levine
Stephen Levine
Raleigh Lieban
Ning Lin
Brenda Lincoln
Judith Lippe
Sylvia S.T. Lo
Lizzy Loeb

Andrew MacLiver
Charles Magee
Kim Magner
Jerry Magnussen
Wilfredo Manalo
Abhijeet Mankar
James Manning
Molly Markert
Dean Martelli
John Martin
Maria Martinez
Joe Masotta
Gerhard Mayer
Maryam Mims
Patrik Moccetti
Rodolfo Modina
Carmen Moore
Anita Moryadas
Paul Murphey

Andrew Naranjo
Staci Nesbitt
Thomas Nohr

Dennis O'Meara
Michio Okamatsu
Jess Oliva
Ronald Oster

Carlo Paganuzzi
Diana Painter
Cynthia Phakos
Chinh Pham
Robert Pigati
George Plazony
Theresa Powell
Haydee Prado
Medina Pruitt

Srinivas Rao
Ian Remulla
Daniel Rhodes
Taina Rikala
Katherine Rinne
Lee Rivera
Jacqueline Rosalagon
Dawn Russ

Tsutomu Sakanaka
Orlando Sanchez
Nanette Sanger
Achille Santos
Albert Sawano
Jennifer Schab
Robert Schaffer

Heidi Schenker
Roy Schmidt
Jeffrey Sessions
Yogesh Seth
Sam Seymour, IV
Rocky Shen
Kevin Sherbrooke
Patricia Shigetomi
Martin Simon
Anson Snyder
Lisa Snyder
Joann Song
Jennifer Spangler
April Spease
Suma Spina
Tom Stallman
J. Odom Stamps
Ralph Stanislaw
Margaret Starcevic
Henry Steinway
Jeffrey Stenfors
Malcolm Stiles
Roy Stuebinger
Wen-Chun Sun
Jan Szupinski

Diana Tasnadi
Charlotte Taylor
Beck Taylor
Leonard Temes
Larry Tighe
Warren Tomashiro
Gertrude Torres
Riccardo Tossani
Mark Tweed
Kevin Tyrrell
Burton Tysinger

Donna Vaccarino
Elena Valderama
Ed Villanueva
Dorian Viniegra
Janet Visconti-Clifton

Phillip Warde
Breton Washington
Allan Weghorst
Michael Wilson
Dianna Wong
Frank Wong
Andrea Woolf
Audrey Wu
Robert Wysinger

Alexander Yahontov
Sui Yao
Yong-Kian Yeo
Alexander Yohontov
Alex Yoo


Mahnam Zarrehparvar
Sarah Zimmerman
Mark Zwagerman

# Chronological List of Buildings & Projects

* Indicates work featured in this book

**\*The New Wilshire (6100 Wilshire)**
Los Angeles, California
Bracton Corporation
1986

1

**\*The City of Kapolei**
Oahu, Hawaii
Estate of James Campbell
1986

**Kapalua Village Hotel, Design Proposal**[1]
Kapalua, Hawaii
Cawn, Rosenzweig Associates
1986

**Park La Brea Master Plan**
Los Angeles, California
Bank of America
1986

2

**MCA Cineplex Parking Structure
and Plaza**[2]
Universal City, California
MCA Development Company
1986

**Rand Corporation**
Santa Monica, California
Rand Corporation
1986

3

**Doheny Plaza**[3]
West Hollywood, California
Lancre International Inc.
1986

**Whittier College, Performing Arts Center Design Proposal**[4]
Whittier, California
Whittier College
1986

**\*Fox Plaza**
Century City, California
MKDG and Twentieth Century Fox Film Corporation
1987

**\*Andrex Vermont Gateway**
Torrance, California
Andrex Development Company
1987

**\*Otis College of Art and Design**
Los Angeles, California
Otis College of Art and Design
1987

**\*University of California at Irvine "Main Street"**
Irvine, California
University of California at Irvine, Office of Physical Planning
1987

**\*Shoshana Wayne Gallery**[5]
Santa Monica, California
Shoshana and Wayne Blank
1987

**UNOCAL Properties**[6]
Brea, California
UNOCAL Properties
1987

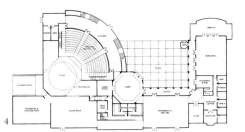

4

5

6

Chronological List
of Buildings & Projects

233

**Paramount Studios Master Plan**
Los Angeles, California
Paramount Pictures Corporation
1987

**Beverly Hills Hotel**
Beverly Hills, California
MKDG
1987

**Whittier College, North Campus
Specific Plan**
Whittier, California
Whittier College
1987

**\*Paradise Restaurant** [7]
Torrance, California
Andrex Development Company
1988

**\*Karl Bornstein Gallery** [8]
Santa Monica, California
Karl Bornstein
1988

**\*Indian Wells Specific Plan** [9]
Indian Wells, California
City of Indian Wells
1988

**Columbia Savings and Loan, Maple Drive
Office Building**
Beverly Hills, California
Columbia Savings and Loan Realty
Advisors
1988

**Columbia Savings and Loan, Wilshire/La Peer Office Building** [10]
Beverly Hills, California
Columbia Savings and Loan
1988

**Schaumberg Convention Center, Master Plan Study**
Schaumberg, Illinois
UNOCAL
1988

**Union Oil Company Master Plan** [11]
Los Angeles, California
UNOCAL
1988

**Calabasas Park Center Master Plan** [12]
Calabasas, California
Ahmanson Commercial Development Company
1988

**Colorado Place Phase III**
Santa Monica, California
Maguire Thomas Partners
1988

**Olympic/Sawtelle Office Building**
Los Angeles, California
Mr Douglas Emmet
1988

**Reagan Library Properties, Master Plan**
Ventura, California
Blakely Swartz Ranch
1988

10

11

12

Chronological List
of Buildings & Projects

235

**Metropolis** [13]
San Diego, California
Tutor Saliba Properties
1988

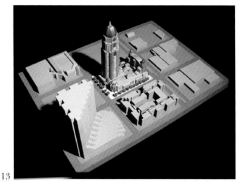
13

**\*Rincon Center**
San Francisco, California
Perini Land and Development Company
1989


**\*Bunker Hill Towers**
Los Angeles, California
First Street Properties
1989


**\*Los Angeles Center**
Los Angeles, California
Hillman Properties West/Smith & Hricik
Urban Development
1989

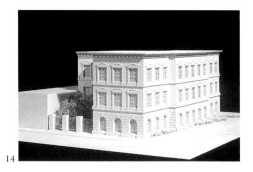
14

**Chartwell Headquarters, Concept Design** [14]
Beverly Hills, California
Chartwell Partnership Group
1989


**Southpark Corporate Center**
Los Angeles, California
Shuwa Investment Corporation
1989


**Giorgio of Beverly Hills** [15]
Beverly Hills, California
Giorgio of Beverly Hills
1989

15

**\*Opus One** [16]
Oakville, California
Baroness Philippine de Rothschild and the
Robert Mondavi Family
1990

16

**\*Pasadena Towers** [17]
Pasadena, California
Ahmanson Commercial Development
Company
1990

**\*1999 Avenue of the Stars**
Century City, California
JMB Urban Development Company
1990

17

**\*6100 Canoga Avenue**
Woodland Hills, California
LaSalle Partners
1990

**\*Rockefeller Center**
New York, New York
Rockefeller Center Management Inc.
1990

**\*Trump Wilshire Tower** [18]
Los Angeles, California
Trump Wilshire Associates
1990

18

**\*Trump Wilshire Center**
Los Angeles, California
Trump Wilshire Associates
1990

Chronological List
of Buildings & Projects

**\*Los Angeles Area Chamber of Commerce Headquarters**
Los Angeles, California
Hillman Properties/Smith & Hricik
1990

19

**\*Nestlé USA Inc. Headquarters** [19]
Glendale, California
Lincoln Properties and Nestlé USA Inc.
1990

**Superconducting Super Collider Laboratories**
Waxahachie, Texas
US Department of Energy
1990

20

**Warner Center** [20]
Los Angeles, California
JMB Urban Development Company
1990

**May Company Adaptive Reuse** [21]
Los Angeles, California
Forest City Development Company
1990

**May Centers, Warner Center**
Los Angeles, California
CenterMark Properties
1990

21

**The Coronet Condominiums**
Beverly Hills, California
The Coronet Condominiums
1990

**\*CNS Resort**
Talofofo, Saipan, Northern Mariana
Islands
Co-You Niizeki Saipan Development
1991

**\*William Morris Rodeo**
Beverly Hills, California
William Morris Agency
1991

**\*Gallo Sonoma Estate Cellars** [22]
Healdsburg, California
Gallo Sonoma Estate Cellars
1991

**\*Pircher House** [23]
Los Angeles, California
Leo and Nina Pircher
1991

**World Trade Center**
Los Angeles, California
Haseko-Dunn California
1991

**Gold Coast Resort** [24]
Queensland Australia
Co-You Corporation
1991

**Whittier College, North Campus
Housing Plan**
Whittier, California
Whittier College
1991

22

23

24

Chronological List
of Buildings & Projects

**\*Pacific Center** [25]
(formerly Pacific Mutual Building)
Los Angeles, California
Pactel Properties, Cushman and Wakefield
1992

**\*Allied Communications Inc.**
Los Angeles, California
Allied Communications Inc.
1992

**\*10880 Wilshire at Westwood** [26]
Westwood, California
Hines Interests Limited Partnership
1992

25

**20th Century Plaza, Warner Ridge Office**
Los Angeles, California
Warner Ridge Associates
1992

**Norton Air Force Base Master Plan**
San Bernardino, California
Inland Valley Development Agency
1992

**Chatsworth Metrolink Station Master Plan**
Chatsworth, California
Los Angeles County Transportation
Commission
1992

26

**\*LeoPalace Resort** [27]
Yona Municipality, Guam
Miyama Development International,
Tokyo
1993

27

**\*SunAmerica Inc. Corporate** [28]
**Headquarters**
Los Angeles, California
SunAmerica Inc.
1993

28

**China Mixed-Use, Schematic Design**
Dalian, China
Bestship Development Ltd
1993

**LACTC Universal City Station Assessment**
Universal City, California
Los Angeles County Metropolitan Transit
Authority
1993

**Beverly Hills Visitors and Cultural Center**
Beverly Hills, California
City of Beverly Hills
1993

29

**\*Union Bank Plaza**
Los Angeles, California
Equitable, NLI
1994

**\*Warner Bros. Office Building** [29]
Burbank, California
Warner Bros.
1994

30

**\*Los Angeles Open Space: A Greenways**
**Plan** [30]
Los Angeles, California
Pacific Earth Resources
1994

**\*"Eye to Eye" Stage Set**
Los Angeles, California
Collage Dance Theatre
1994


**\*Private House** [31]
St Helena, California
Scott Johnson, Margaret Bates
1994


**\*Warner Bros. Telepictures** [32]
Burbank, California
Warner Bros.
1994


**FEMA Emergency Housing Project**
Dededo, Guam
Federal Emergency Management Act,
Guam Housing Corporation
1994


**Lada Housing Estates, Affordable Housing Project**
Dededo, Guam
Guam Housing Corporation, GovGuam
1994


**NBC Studios, Jay Leno ("Tonight Show") Stage** [33]
Burbank, California
National Broadcasting Corporation
1994


**People's Construction Bank of China**
Beijing, China
People's Construction Bank of China,
Beijing Branch
1994

31

32

33

**\*Warner Bros. Technical Operations**
Burbank, California
Warner Bros.
1995


**\*Patramas Adhiloka Oil Plaza** [34]
Jakarta, Indonesia
Pt. Patramas Adhiloka
1995


**\*Sunflower City** [35]
Bangkok, Thailand
The Sunflower Group
1995


**\*Al-Khobar Resort Hotel** [36]
Al-Khobar, Saudi Arabia
Al-Obiayi Contracting & Maintenance
Company
1995


**\*DreamWorks SKG**
Playa Vista, California
Maguire Thomas Partners,
DreamWorks SKG
1995


**Dededo Master Plan, Land for the
Landless**
Dededo, Guam
Guam Housing Corporation, GovGuam
1995


**Los Angeles International Airport
Master Plan**
Los Angeles, California
City of Los Angeles Department of Airports
1995

34

35

36

**Martyr Street Office, Interiors**
Agana, Guam
Calvo Enterprises
1995


**Digital Magic**
Santa Monica, California
Four Media Company
1995

**Four Media Company Office Building** [37]
Los Angeles, California
Four Media Company
1995


**1880 Century Park East**
Century City, California
Held Properties
1995

**1888 Century Park East** [38]
Century City, California
JMB Urban Development Company
1995

**Commerce Casino** [39]
City of Commerce, California
Commerce Casino Inc.
1995


**Amgen Inc. Master Plan**
Thousand Oaks, California
Amgen Inc.
1995

**Amgen Inc. Building 27**
Thousand Oaks, California
Amgen Inc.
1995

**Camp Amgen Inc., Temporary Facility**
Thousand Oaks, California
Amgen Inc.
1995

**Carsey-Werner Productions,
Design Concept**
Culver City, California
Carsey-Werner Productions
1995

**\*Los Angeles Civic Center
Enhancement Plan** [40]
Los Angeles, California
Los Angeles Civic Center Authority
1996

**\*All Saints' Parish**
Beverly Hills, California
All Saints' Parish
1996

**\*Byron Winery** [41]
Santa Maria Valley, California
Byron Vineyard and Winery
1996

**\*Pacific Corporate Towers** [42]
El Segundo, California
CB Commercial, GE Capital Investment
Advisors
1996

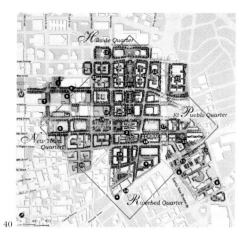

40

41

42

Chronological List
of Buildings & Projects

**\*Valencia Town Center Office Building** [(43)]
Valencia, California
Newhall Land and Farming Company
1996

**\*Marlborough School** [(44)]
Los Angeles, California
Marlborough School
1996

**\*Johnson Fain Partners Office**
Los Angeles, California
Johnson Fain Partners
1996

43

**\*Queensway Bay Parking Garage** [(45)]
Queensway Bay, Long Beach, California
City of Long Beach
1996

**\*Fox Canopies**
Los Angeles, California
LaSalle Partners
1996

44

**RAMA IX Square** [(46)]
Bangkok, Thailand
Praram IX Square Ltd
1996

**Los Angeles County Museum of Art
Expansion Study**
Los Angeles, California
Los Angeles County Museum of Art
1996

45

**NBC Studios Master Plan**
Burbank, California
National Broadcasting Company Inc.
1996

**Amgen Inc. Parking Structure 3**
Thousand Oaks, California
Amgen Inc.
1996

**Amgen Inc. Operations Facilities
Master Plan**
Thousand Oaks, California
Amgen Inc.
1996

**Twentieth Century Insurance
Headquarters** [47]
Woodland Hills, California
Twentieth Century Insurance
1996

**Happy Landing Road**
Location Tumon, Guam
Toyo Real Estate Company
1996

**Guam International Airport Master Plan
and Base Reuse Plan** [48]
Tamuning, Guam
Guam Airport Authority
1996

**Satpon Point Planning**
Tamuning, Guam
Toyo Real Estate Company
1996

46

47

48

Chronological List                    247
of Buildings & Projects

**Century City Parking Lot 7a** [49]
Century City, California
JMB Urban Development Company
1996

**Valencia Town Center Building II**
Valencia, California
Newhall Land and Farming Company
1996

**University of Science and Technology
Master Plan** [50]
Pattaya, Thailand
University of Science and Technology
1996

**\*Mission Bay Master Plan** [51]
San Francisco, California
Catellus Development Corporation
1997

**Amgen Inc. Process Development
Laboratories (Building 30)** [52]
Thousand Oaks, California
Amgen Inc.
1997

**Broadway Department Store State
Office Building** [53]
Los Angeles, California
Los Angeles State Building Authority
1997

**Warner Bros. International
Recreation Enterprises**
Glendale, California
Warner Bros.
1997

49

50

51

**Byron Winery Visitors' Center**
Santa Maria Valley, California
Byron Vineyard and Winery
1997

**Gooden Residence**
Malibu, California
Mr and Mrs John Gooden
1997

52

**Valencia Town Center Building III**
Valencia, California
Newhall Land and Farming Company
1997

53

# Recent Design Awards

## Architecture

**Gold Nugget Award of Merit**
Public/Private Special Use Facility
Byron Winery
Santa Maria, California
1997

**Gold Nugget Award of Merit**
Office/Professional Buildings
Los Angeles Area Chamber of Commerce
Los Angeles, California
1997

**Gold Nugget Award of Merit**
Custom Home
Private Residence
St Helena, California
1997

**Urban Beautification Award**
New Commercial Mid-Rise
Los Angeles Business Council
Warner Brothers Office Building
Burbank, California
1996

**Best Rehabilitation and Modernization**
Building Owners and Management
Association
Union Bank Plaza
Los Angeles, California
1995

**Gold Nugget Award of Merit**
Best Office/Professional Building
Pasadena Towers
Pasadena, California
1994

**Los Angeles Beautiful Business and
Industry Award for Architecture**
Los Angeles Business Council
1999 Avenue of the Stars
Century City, California
1993

**Special Recognition Award**
Precast/Prestressed Concrete Institute
William Morris Rodeo
Beverly Hills, California
1993

**Citation in Architectural Conservation**
Buildings, Facilities and Construction
Management
Foundation for San Francisco's
Architectural Heritage
Rincon Center
San Francisco, California
1992

**Los Angeles Beautiful Business and
Industry Award for Architecture**
Los Angeles Business Council
Nestlé USA Inc. Headquarters
Glendale, California
1991

**Merit Award**
California Preservation Foundation
Rincon Center
San Francisco, California
1989

**Los Angeles Beautiful Business and
Industry Award**
Fox Plaza
Century City, California
1987

**Beautification Award**
West Los Angeles Chamber of Commerce
Fox Plaza
Century City, California
1986

**Design Award**
Los Angeles Chapter AIA
Tom Bradley International Terminal, LAX
1984

**Design Award**
Orange County Chapter AIA
Yamaha Motor Corp., USA
Torrance, California
1984

**Citation Honor Award**
Los Angeles Chapter AIA
Fred L. Hartley Research Center, Union
Oil Company
Los Angeles, California
1984

**Design Excellence Award**
California Building Officials
Toyota Motor Sales USA, Inc.
Torrance, California
1983

## Urban Design

**"Citation" Award for Urban Design**
Progressive Architecture
Los Angeles Open Space:
A Greenways Plan
Los Angeles, California
1994

**Urban Design Citation**
Los Angeles Chapter AIA
Los Angeles Open Space: A Greenways
Plan
Los Angeles, California
1993

**Gold Nugget Merit Award**
Best Community Site Plan
Leopalace Resort
Guam
1992

**Gold Nugget Merit Award**
Best New Town Land Plan
Ewa Town Center, Kapolei
Oahu, Hawaii
1992

**National AIA Citation for Excellence in
Urban Design**
Indian Wells Specific Plan
Indian Wells, California
1990

**Award**
Progressive Architecture
Indian Wells Specific Plan
Indian Wells, California
1989

**Urban Design Citation**
Los Angeles Chapter AIA
Indian Wells Specific Plan
Indian Wells, California
1989

**National AIA Citation for Excellence in
Urban Design**
University of California at Irvine
"Main Street"
Irvine, California
1989

**Award**
Progressive Architecture
University of California at Irvine "Main
Street"
Irvine, California
1988

**Design Award**
California Council AIA
Ewa Town Center, Kapolei
Oahu, Hawaii
1987

# Milestone Projects of William L. Pereira Associates

**UC San Diego Central Library**
San Diego, California
University of California, San Diego

**Los Angeles International Airport Master Plan[1]**
Los Angeles, California
City of Los Angeles

**Pepperdine University**
Malibu, California
Pepperdine University

**University of California at Irvine Master Plan**
Irvine, California
Regents of the University of California

**Irvine Ranch Master Plan**
Irvine, California
The Irvine Company

**Doha Sheraton Hotel & Conference Center**
Doha, Qatar
State of Qatar

**New District of Doha**
Doha, Qatar
State of Qatar

**Medical Center of Iran**
Teheran, Iran
Government of Iran

**CBS Television City[2]**
Los Angeles, California
Columbia Broadcasting System

**Citicorp Center**
San Francisco, California
Citibank NA

**Lockheed Corporate Headquarters**
Calabasas, California
Lockheed Corporation

**Union Oil Center[2]**
Los Angeles, California
Union Oil Company of California

**Los Angeles County Museum of Art**
Los Angeles, California
Museum Associates

**Woodlands New Community[3]**
Houston, Texas
George P. Mitchell & Associates

**American Airlines Headquarters**
Dallas/Fort Worth Airport, Texas
Dallas/Fort Worth Regional Airport

**Tom Bradley International Terminal[4]**
Los Angeles International Airport
City of Los Angeles

**Transamerica Headquarters**
San Francisco, California
Transamerica Corporation

1  Pereira & Luckman, with Welton Becket & Associates and Paul R. Williams
2  Pereira & Luckman
3  In association with Robert Gladstone Associates, Richard P. Browne Associates, and Wallace, McHarg, Roberts & Todd
4  Pereira-Dworsky-Sinclair-Williams joint venture

# Publications

## Books

Frantz, Douglas. *From the Ground Up, The Business of Building in the Age of Money.* Berkeley: University of California Press, 1991.

Hirschman, Jessica Elin. *For Your Home: Paint & Color.* New York: Michael Friedman Publishing Group, 1993.

King, Carol Soucek. *At Home and at Work.* New York: PBC International, 1993.

Miller, Sam F. *Design Process: A Primer for Architectural and Interior Designers.* New York: Van Nostrand Reinhold, 1995.

## Journal articles

"3-D CAD System Generates Complex Dome Design." *PC Times* (April 1, 1991).

"35th Annual P/A Awards: UC Irvine Main Street." *Progressive Architecture* (January 1988).

"36th Annual P/A Awards: Highway 111." *Progressive Architecture* (January 1989).

"Architect by Design." *Los Angeles Business Journal* (June 3–9, 1991).

"Australia — Magnum Opus." *Belle* (February/March 1993).

"The Best Wine Ever (Opus One Winery)." *San Francisco Examiner* (October 13, 1991).

"Building on Open Systems." *Uniform Monthly* (February 1992).

"Business by Design." *California Business* (May 1989).

"Carnation Picks Glendale." *Los Angeles Times* (May 29, 1988).

"The Changing Western Home." *Sunset* (April 1993).

"A Corporate and Public Garden." *Urban Land* (July 1993).

"County's Space Odyssey Keys On More Greenways." *Los Angeles Business Journal* (October 26, 1992).

"Decision Looms on Fate of Norton Air Base." *Los Angeles Business Journal* (November 23, 1992).

"Designs for the Southland Puzzle (Highway 111)." *Los Angeles Times* (February 5, 1989).

"Eighth Century Domes Built with 20th Century CAD." *Microcad News* (May 1991).

"Greenway Plan for Los Angeles." *Progressive Architecture* (January 1994).

"Hearth and Harmony." *Los Angeles Times Magazine* (October 25, 1992).

"Hong Kong — Magnum Opus." *The Peak* (October 1992).

"Interior Design Honor Award." *Sunset* (October 1992).

Interview with Scott Johnson. *PSA Magazine* (September 1987).

"Japanese Leisure Means Work for Architects." *Los Angeles Business Journal* (November 27 – December 3, 1989).

"JFPA: In L.A. It's a Hot Architect." *Engineering News-Record* (June 7, 1990).

"Light and Color (Pircher Residence)." Self (September 1994).

"Mantel." *Remodeling* (February 1993).

"The New Urban Design: The Ewa Town Center." *Progressive Architecture* (March 1988).

"Opus One Project Will Be Testament to 2 Wine Makers." *Los Angeles Times* (July 17, 1988).

"Opus One Winery." *Designers West* (November 1992),

"Opus One Winery." *Redwood News* (Fall/Winter 1992).

"Opus One." *Wine Spectator* (November 15, 1995).

"Orderly Succession for Heirs to L.A.'s King of Architecture." *Los Angeles Times* (May 19, 1988).

"A Partnership That's Ripe With Collaboration." *Los Angeles Times* (July 12, 1990).

"Perfect Blend: The Opus One Winery Marries Two Architectural Traditions." *Interiors* (February 1993).

"Private Residence in Napa Valley." *Appelation Wine Country Living* (April/May 1997).

"Private Residence in Napa Valley." *Architectural Digest* (March 1996).

"Private Residence in Napa Valley." *Deutsche Bauzeitschrift* (July 1996).

"Private Residence in Napa Valley." *Interiors* (May 1996).

"Rare Vintage: Opus One Winery." *Architectural Record* (May 1992).

"Reading Rooms." *Home* (February 1992).

"Renaissance Man." *Designers West* (May 1989).

"Rincon Center." *Urban Land* (August 1992).

"Rooms at the Top." *Avenue* (March 1989).

"Scott Johnson's Main Chance." *Los Angeles Times Magazine* (November 24, 1991).

"Skyline Addition (Nestlé U.S.A.)" *Designers West* (February 1992).

"Suns, Stars and AutoCAD." *CADalyst* (May 1991).

"Synergy." *SunWorld* (November 1991).

"Wilshire Boulevard: The Artery That Brings Life Blood to L.A." *Daily Commerce* (April 30, 1991).

"Work Begins on HQ for L.A. Chamber of Commerce." *Los Angeles Business Journal* (September 23, 1991).

# Acknowledgments

We wish to thank Anita Moryadas for her graphic design and editorial contributions to this book, and her supervision of the production team. Additional thanks go to Kim Colin for coordinating artwork and photography, Sui Yao for assisting in the compilation, Loretta Lee for drawing preparation, and Mark Gershen for research and archival support. We also wish to thank the Images Publishing Group for their invitation to participate in this series.

## Consultants

### Landscape Architects
Belt Collins
Peter Brandow & Associates
Campbell & Campbell
Closson & Closson, Inc.
Marcia Babalas Design
Meléndrez Associates
Olin Partnership
Olson Associates
Peridian, International
Pod, Inc.
Robert Herrick Carter & Associates
Robert Joseph Clark Associates
Royston Hanamoto Alley & Abey
Martha Schwartz, Inc.
Tongg Clarke & Mechler
Emmet L. Wemple & Associates
WMRT

### Golf Course Architects
Jack Nicklaus Golf Services
Palmer Course Design Company

### Structural Engineers
Brandow & Johnston
Cbm Engineers, Inc.
Chin & Hensolt Engineers, Inc.
Robert Engelkirk
Erkel, Greenfield & Associates
John A. Martin & Associates
Kpff
Nabih Yousef & Associates
Ronald L. Rogahn
Tibor Ginter Structural Engineer, Inc.
Wong Hobach Lau

### Mechanical/Electrical/Plumbing Consultants
Kim Casey & Harase, Inc.
Levine/Seegel Associates
Patsouras & Associates
Syska & Hennessy

### Acoustical Consultants
Bolt, Beranek and Newman, Inc.
Bruce Davy & Associates
Mckay Conant Brook
Paoletti Associates
Paul S. Veneklasen and Associates
Purcell + Noppe + Associates, Inc.

### Lighting Consultants
Childs Associates
Gotham Light & Power
Horton-Lees Lighting Design, Inc.
Francis Krahe & Associates
J. Craig Roberts Associates

### Graphics/Signage
Michael Manwaring
Paul Hershfield Designs
Ralph Bennett Associates
Sussman/Prejza & Company, Inc.

### Photographers
Charles Callister
Erich Koyama
Mark Lohman
Mary Nichols
Erhard Pfeiffer
Tim Street-Porter
Adrian Vilicescu
Stephen Whittaker
Annette del Zoppo

### Model Makers
Architectural Models
Dimensional Presentations, Inc.
Model Concepts, Inc.
Scale Models Unlimited

### Artists (Renderings)
Michael Abbot
William Block
Jeffrey A. Crussell Associates
Designers Ink, Anthony Van Strauhal
Al Forster
Hank Hockenberger
Doug Jameson
Petko Kadiev
Tibor Karsai
Norm Kondy, AIA
Jon Messer
Lawrence E. Perron
Human Tan
Eric Van Der Palen
Barry Zauss

## Photography credits
Joe Aker: 105 (3); 106 (4–6); 107 (8–10)
Charles Callister Jr.: 146 (1); 148 (7); 150 (12)
Edmund Einy: 134 (1); 135 (1–3)
John Gaylord: 47 (4)
Paula Goldman: 93 (12)
Chris Howell: 86 (7)
Kirk S. Irwin: 143 (7); 145 (12)
Erich Koyama: 50 (1,2); 51 (3,4); 52 (10,11); 53 (13)
Tom Lamb: 52 (8,9,12)
Mark Lohman: 28 (1); 29 (2–5); 30 (6,7); 31 (10,11); 42 (1); 43 (2,3); 44 (5–8); 45 (10–12) 56 (1); 57 (2,3); 60 (1); 62 (4-6); 64 (1,2); 65 (4); 66 (2); 67 (3-7); 68 (8-11); 82 (17,18); 83 (19-21); 98 (6,8); 99 (10,11); 108 (4,5); 110 (2-4); 116 (2); 125 (3,6); 141 (3); 146 (2); 152 (1); 153 (2); 154 (4-6); 155 (7); 163 (2,3); 165 (6,7); 170 (10-13); 171 (14); 177 (2); 184 (1); 185 (2-4); 202 (1-3); 203 (4)
Barry Michlin: 136 (1); 137 (2-5)
Mary E. Nichols: 161 (12,13)
Erhard Pfeiffer: Cover (Fox Canopies) 30 (8); 37 (20); 48 (6); 49 (8,9); 54 (1); 55 (2,3); 74 (2); 75 (3-5); 76 (6,7); 102 (1-3); 103 (4-7); 108 (1–3); 109 (6); 110 (1); 112 (7); 113 (8,9); 114 (11); 115 (12-15); 120 (1); 121 (2-6); 130 (1,2); 131 (4,5); 132 (6); 133 (8,9); 140 (1); 141 (2); 142 (4); 143 (5,6); 144 (8); 145 (9-11); 147 (3); 156 (1,2); 157 (3); 158 (5,6); 159 (7-10); 160 (11); 172 (all); 173 (all); 174 (all); 175 (all); 186 (6,7); 187 (8); 188 (9); 189 (10,11); 190 (1); 191 (2,3); 200 (1); 201 (2); 204 (1,2); 205 (3-5); 206 (1); 207 (2-5); 208 (6,7); 209 (8-12); 210 (1); 211 (2,3); 212 (2); 213 (4,5,8); 214 (1-3); 215 (4-6); 216 (1); 217 (2,5)
Tim Street-Porter: 147 (4); 148 (6-9); 149 (10,11); 151 (14,15); 192 (1); 193 (2,3); 194 (5,6); 195 (7,8); 196–199 (all)
Adrian Velicscu: 58 (1–4); 59 (5–8)
Jay Venezia: 116 (1); 117 (3-6); 118 (7); 119 (11-13)
Steve Whittaker: 32 (1,2); 33 (3–5); 34 (7); 35 (12–15); 36 (16–18); 37 (21)
Annette del Zoppo: 89 (9)

## Renderer credits
Andy Cox: 128 (6); 129 (7–9)
Al Forster: 130 (3)
Hank Hockenberger: 69 (12,13); 86 (9); 87 (10-12); 166 (12); 167 (3-5); 168 (6); 169 (7-9)
Norman Kondy: 80 (12,13); 81 (14–16); 98 (9); 100 (12,13); 101 (14,15)
Joseph Massotta 44 (9)
Jon Messer: 78 (1)
Lawrence Perron: 63 (7); 77 (8–11)

# Index

Every effort has been made to trace the original source of copyright material contained in this book. The publishers would be pleased to hear from copyright holders to rectify any errors or omissions.

The information and illustrations in this publication have been prepared and supplied by Johnson Fain Partners. While all reasonable efforts have been made to ensure accuracy, the publishers do not, under any circumstances, accept responsibility for errors, omissions and representations express or implied.